PEERCOIN

PROOF OF STAKE
PIONEERS

2012-2013-2014-2015-2016-2017-2018-2019
A CONCISE PEERCOIN HISTORY BOOK

Peercoin—Proof of Stake Pioneers

by Christopher P. Thompson

Book Author by Christopher P. Thompson

Book Design by C. Ellis

ISBN—9781093658316

PEERCOIN

PROOF OF STAKE PIONEERS

2012-2013-2014-2015-2016-2017-2018-2019
A CONCISE PEERCOIN HISTORY BOOK

CHRISTOPHER P. THOMPSON

CONTENTS

CONTENTS

INTRODUCTION

Since the inception of Bitcoin in 2008, thousands of cryptocurrencies or decentralised blockchains have been launched. Most ventures into the cryptocurrency sphere have not gone according to plan as their founders would have hoped. Nevertheless, there are currently hundreds of crypto related projects which are succeeding.

This book covers the history of Peercoin, a decentralised, globally accessible and secure ecosystem for transferring value across the world. Since August 2012, a growing committed and visionary team of developers has been driving the project forward. Major events which have occurred since the blockchain launched on the 19th August 2012 include:

- First Peercoin proof of stake block was timestamped (SEPTEMBER 2012)

- PPCoin blockchain switched to version 0.3 protocol code (MARCH 2013)

- Peercoin logo designed, unveiled and adopted (JULY 2013)

- Peercoin blockchain switched to version 0.4 protocol code (MAY 2014)

- Peercoin blockchain switched to version 0.5 protocol code (APRIL 2016)

- Peercoin rebranded (SEPTEMBER 2016)

- First PPC RFC protocol improvement proposal submitted (JANUARY 2017)

- Peercoin blockchain switched to version 0.6 protocol code (DECEMBER 2017)

- All time 2012-2018 high USD fiat price per PPC recorded (JANUARY 2018)

- Peercoin Foundation was established (MAY 2018)

- Peercoin blockchain switched to version 0.7 protocol code (MARCH 2019)

INTRODUCTION

To be specific, this book covers a concise chronological series of events from the 10th August 2012 to the 12th March 2019. During this time, Peercoin has attracted growing interest from inside and outside the cryptocurrency space.

You may have bought this book because Peercoin, PPC, is your favourite cryptographic blockchain. Alternatively, you may be keen to find out how it all began. I have presented the information henceforth without going into too much technical discussion. If you would like to investigate further, I recommend that you read material currently available at https://peercoin.net

If you choose to purchase a certain amount of PPC, please do not buy more than you can afford to lose.

Enjoy the book :D

WHAT IS PEERCOIN?

Peercoin is a cryptocurrency or digital decentralised currency. It is described as the world's first energy efficient, secure and sustainable blockchain. Peercoin wallet users can send PPC anywhere in the world without the need to trust a central authority. Cryptography has been implemented and coded into the network allowing the user to send currency through a decentralised (no central point of failure), open source (anyone can review the code), peer-to-peer network.

Peercoin began in October 2011. During ten months of research and discovery, Sunny King and Scott Nadal invented and introduced the proof of stake timestamping consensus mechanism. After making significant modifications to Bitcoin, Peercoin launched on the 19th August 2012. It was the first cryptocurrency of its kind to use proof of stake timestamping to secure decentralisation alongside proof of work, which distributed the majority of PPC.

> "When Sunny King originally developed Peercoin, he had a very specific long-term vision of a network that is designed for maximum decentralisation and security. Peercoin's underlying purpose is to provide the ability to store value in an inexpensive to maintain crypto network which prioritises security, decentralisation and scarcity over speed, low fees and high transaction volumes. This is the definition of a back-bone currency."

Since its launch, the Peercoin blockchain has achieved many milestones. A talented development team is responsible for maintaining and expanding its functionalities via the implementation of hard forks and innovative second-layer protocols. For example, PeerAssets and Perpera are two currently active projects.

The slogan used by Peercoin to market the blockchain is:

"THE WORLD'S FIRST EFFICIENT AND SUSTAINABLE PUBLIC BLOCKCHAIN"

WHY USE PEERCOIN?

Like all cryptocurrencies, people have chosen to utilise Peercoin as a medium of exchange or store of value through personal choice. An innovative feature of the coin, an affinity towards the brand or high confidence in the competency of the development team could be reasons why. Key benefits of using Peercoin include:

- All transactions are automatically validated and processed by the protocol code software.

- It is accessible from anywhere in the world via the Internet.

- No third parties need to be trusted to verify transactions.

- It is free from government censorship or other third party interference.

- It is immutable so no third parties are able to falsify or remove transactions.

- It is immune from the effects of hyperinflation.

- It has no central point of failure.

- Wallet users receive block reward incentives for securing the network.

IS PEERCOIN MONEY?

Money is a form of acceptable, convenient and valued medium of payment for goods and services within an economy. It allows two parties to exchange goods or services without the need to barter. This eradicates the potential situation where one party of the two may not want what the other has to offer. The main properties of money are:

- **As a medium of exchange**—money can be used as a means to buy/sell goods/services without the need to barter.

- **A unit of account**—a common measure of value wherever one is in the world.

- **Portable**—easily transferred from one party to another. The medium used can be easily carried.

- **Durable**—all units of the currency can be lost, but not destroyed.

- **Divisible**—each unit can be subdivided into smaller fractions of that unit.

- **Fungible**— each unit of account is the same as every other unit within the medium (1 PPC = 1 PPC).

- **As a store of value**—it sustains its purchasing power (what it can buy) over long periods of time.

Peercoin easily satisfies the first six characteristics. Taking into account the last characteristic, the value of Peercoin, like all currencies, comes from people willing to accept it as a medium of exchange. Additionally, it must be a secure way to store personal wealth. As it gets adopted by more individuals or merchants, its intrinsic value will increase accordingly.

COIN SPECIFICATION

At the time of publication of this book, its current specification is:

Unit of Account:	PPC
Time of Announcement:	10th August 2012 at 14:18:31 UTC
Time of Blockchain Launch:	19th August 2012 at 18:19:16 UTC
Founders:	Sunny King and Scott Nadal
Project Leader:	Peerchemist
Brand Manager:	Sentinelrv
Community Manager:	Buckkets
Hashing Algorithm:	SHA-256
Timestamping Algorithm:	Hybrid PoW/PoS
Total Coins:	No limit (2-3% inflation)
Block Time:	10 minutes
Transaction Fee:	0.01 PPC per kB
Minimum Stake Age:	30 days
Maximum Stake Age:	90 days
Pre-mine:	None

MILESTONE TIMELINE

10th August 2012	—PPCoin blockchain announced at 14:18:31 UTC
16th August 2012	—PPCoin version 0.1.0 was released
19th August 2012	—Original PPCoin Design Paper was published
19th August 2012	—PPCoin blockchain launched at 18:19:16 UTC
26th August 2012	—Sunny King posted his first weekly update
26th August 2012	—First official PPCoin forum opened
10th August 2012	—PPCoin version 0.2.0 was released
4th September 2012	—First exchange called Cryptocoin initiated PPC trading
7th September 2012	—Bitparking exchange initiated PPC trading
18th September 2012	—First PoS block of the PPCoin blockchain timestamped
18th September 2012	—First PPCoin block explorer went live
18th September 2012	—PPCoin version 0.2.1 was released
3rd October 2012	—Over 10,000,000 PPC generated to date
11th November 2012	—PPCoin version 0.2.2 was released
18th November 2012	—Vircurex exchange initiated PPC trading
26th December 2012	—Over 15,000,000 PPC generated to date

2013

9th February 2013	—First fork of the PPCoin blockchain launched
16th February 2013	—PPCoin version 0.3.0 was released
4th March 2013	—First official PPCoin Facebook page was created
19th March 2013	—Revamped official PPCoin forum went live
20th March 2013	—PPCoin blockchain switched to version 0.3.0 protocol
6th April 2013	—BTC-e exchange initiated PPC trading
24th April 2013	—Bter exchange initiated PPC trading
28th April 2013	—PPCoin added to www.coinmarketcap.com

MILESTONE TIMELINE

2nd May 2013	—Second PPCoin fork BitBar launched
8th May 2013	—Third PPCoin fork YACoin launched
16th May 2013	—Fourth PPCoin fork Bitgem launched
23rd May 2013	—Cryptsy exchange initiated PPC trading
28th May 2013	—Crypto Trade exchange initiated PPC trading
22nd June 2013	—Coins-e exchange initiated PPC trading
27th June 2013	—99Designs Peercoin Logo Contest began
28th June 2013	—Sunny King announced Primecoin
7th July 2013	—Primecoin blockchain launched at 18:28:00 UTC
13th July 2013	—New Peercoin logo design adopted
8th August 2013	—Sunny King was interviewed by Vitalik Buterin
16th August 2013	—Over 20,000,000 PPC generated to date
19th September 2013	—mcxNOW exchange initiated PPC trading
28th September 2013	—Jordan Lee introduced Peershares
30th September 2013	—CoinEX exchange initiated PPC trading
19th October 2013	—First Sunny King community interview took place
28th October 2013	—Vault of Satoshi exchange initiated PPC trading
4th November 2013	—Peercoin Twitter @PeercoinPPC was created
18th November 2013	—PPC attained parity with the USD for the first time
30th November 2013	—All time 2013 high Peercoin market cap recorded
4th December 2013	—First Peercoin promotional video produced

2014

3rd January 2014	—All time 2014 high Peercoin market cap recorded
29th January 2014	—Bittylicious exchange initiated PPC trading
9th February 2014	—Peershares logo designs unveiled and accepted

MILESTONE TIMELINE

13th February 2014	—Bittrex exchange initiated PPC trading
16th February 2014	—Peer4commit website went live
5th April 2014	—Peercoin version 0.4 was released
8th April 2014	—Poloniex exchange initiated PPC trading
22nd April 2014	—The Rock Trading exchange initiated PPC trading
13th May 2014	—Coinnext exchange initiated PPC trading
30th May 2014	—Peerunity version 0.1.0 was released
5th June 2014	—Jordan Lee announced the NuBits project
7th June 2014	—Peerchemist announced Peerbox
17th June 2014	—Sigmike became a Peercoin core developer
18th June 2014	—CCEDK exchange initiated PPC trading
30th June 2014	—Peercoin Marketing Fund launched
10th July 2014	—Chronos Crypto uploaded his first Peercoin video
26th August 2014	—Peerbox logo design was published
11th September 2014	—First Peercoin Android wallet was released
23rd September 2014	—NuBits blockchain launched
11th October 2014	—Peerunity version 0.1.1 was released
6th December 2014	—Cryptopia initiated PPC trading

2015

1st January 2015	—Peercoin annualised inflation recorded at 4.71%
19th January 2015	—New Peerunity wallet client design theme proposed
20th May 2015	—Peercoin first year history book published on Amazon
6th September 2015	—The Peercoin CryptoID block explorer went live
9th November 2015	—Peercoin blockchain suffered a fork issue
8th December 2015	—Peercoin version 0.4.2 was released

MILESTONE TIMELINE

2016

15th January 2016	—Cryptsy exchange ceased PPC trading
5th March 2016	—Peercoin version 0.5.2 was released
10th March 2016	—All time 2016 high PPC market capitalisation attained
21st March 2016	—Peercoin version 0.5.3 was released
26th March 2016	—Peerunity version 0.2.0 was released
6th April 2016	—LiteBit exchange initiated PPC trading
26th April 2016	—Peercoin switched to version 0.5 code protocol
27th April 2016	—Peerunity version 0.2.1 was released
6th May 2016	—Peercoin version 0.5.4 was released
6th May 2016	—Peerunity version 0.2.2 was released
6th May 2016	—Peerchemist published the Peerassets whitepaper
14th June 2016	—Southxchange exchange initiated PPC trading
14th July 2016	—CoinDesk interviewed the Peercoin team
6th August 2016	—Peerchemist created http://chat.peerbox.me
19th August 2016	—Peercoin presence on Beyond Bitcoin Radio Show
13th September 2016	—Superppc purchased the www.peercoin.org address
16th September 2016	—New Peercoin logo design adopted
28th October 2016	—Official Peercoin Telegram chat group created
7th December 2016	—Peercoin Twitter account surpassed 5,000 followers

2017

4th January 2017	—RFC-0001 protocol improvement proposal submitted
14th January 2017	—Peercoin forum went live at https://talk.peercoin.net
10th February 2017	—First Peercoin team update was posted

MILESTONE TIMELINE

7th March 2017	—First Peerassets DAC called Indicium pre-announced
22nd March 2017	—RFC-0002 protocol improvement proposal submitted
22nd March 2017	—RFC-0003 protocol improvement proposal submitted
5th April 2017	—Peerchemist became Peercoin Project Leader
17th May 2017	—RFC-0004 protocol improvement proposal submitted
25th June 2017	—Peercoin Twitter account surpassed 10,000 followers
25th July 2017	—Indicium logo designs unveiled
27th July 2017	—BTC-e exchange shutdown
17th August 2017	—HitBTC exchange initiated PPC trading
20th October 2017	—Bitsane exchange initiated PPC trading
25th October 2017	—Peercoin version 0.6.0 was released
7th November 2017	—Peercoin version 0.6.1 was released
20th November 2017	—RFC-0005 protocol improvement proposal submitted
21st November 2017	—RFC-0006 protocol improvement proposal submitted
18th December 2017	—All time 2017 high PPC market capitalisation attained
20th December 2017	—Peercoin version 0.6 soft fork hit 90% adoption
20th December 2017	—Peercoin blockchain switched to version 0.6 protocol
22nd December 2017	—Livecoin exchange initiated PPC trading

2018

13th January 2018	—All time 2018 high PPC market capitalisation attained
13th February 2018	—Modern PPC paper wallet address generator released
11th March 2018	—Peercoin version 0.6.2 was released
3rd April 2018	—Official Peercoin Discord channel was created
23rd April 2018	—Peercoin version 0.6.3 was released
8th May 2018	—Peercoin announced partnership with StakeBox

MILESTONE TIMELINE

14th May 2018	—Peercoin Foundation established
16th May 2018	—RFC-0007 protocol improvement proposal submitted
16th May 2018	—RFC-0008 protocol improvement proposal submitted
16th May 2018	—RFC-0010 protocol improvement proposal submitted
22nd May 2018	—Ledger Nano S began to officially support Peercoin
5th September 2018	—Peercoin version 0.6.4 was released
14th September 2018	—Kompler exchange initiated PPC trading
17th September 2018	—Coin Switch initiated PPC trading
21st September 2018	—Peercoin was added to Blockfolio Signal
23rd September 2018	—First Peercoin Foundation board meeting occurred
26th October 2018	—Peercoin went live on Delta Direct
31st October 2018	—Project Perpera announced
9th November 2018	—RFC-0011 protocol improvement proposal submitted

2019

7th January 2019	—Revamped official Peercoin website went live
8th January 2019	—BitTurk exchange initiated PPC trading
15th January 2019	—Amsterdex exchange initiated PPC trading
22nd January 2019	—Peercoin version 0.7.0 was released
17th February 2019	—Peercoin version 0.7.1 was released
20th February 2019	—BC Bitcoin exchange initiated PPC trading
26th February 2019	—Peercoin version 0.8 testing began
12th March 2019	—Peercoin blockchain switched to v0.7 code protocol

BLOCKCHAIN

Blockchain technology was introduced to the world when Satoshi Nakamoto published the Bitcoin whitepaper in October 2008. Since that time, the concept of blockchain has grown, advanced and proliferated. It has the potential to impact society in innumerable realised and unforeseen ways.

By improving the Bitcoin codebase, Sunny King innovatively introduced a brand new timestamping consensus mechanism called proof of stake (see page 22). It is the method by which the Peercoin blockchain sustains its decentralised security.

A blockchain is usually described as a distributed public ledger of all transactions (contained within blocks) ever executed since the first block. Unlike relying on third parties to record financial transactions, trust is automatically enforced by decentralised code protocol. A large group of node holders (validators) hosting full copies of the blockchain are collectively responsible for validating transactions, which are then grouped together in a block every ten minutes or so. Blocks are added to the blockchain in such a manner that each block contains the hash of the prior one. It is therefore utterly resistant to modification. Consequently, the problem of double-spending is solved.

> "Each security validator has the ability to independently verify the ledger's integrity. In this way the public ledger acts as a digitally shared truth about the state of the network"

Since the launch of the Peercoin blockchain, the number of transactions and blocks has continuously grown. Each wallet client user's account balance automatically updates without the risk of error, potential fraud or censorship.

What follows is the first block timestamped to the Peercoin blockchain:

Block #1 (Reward 2,499.75 PPC) August 19th 2012 at 18:19:16 UTC

BLOCKCHAIN

As a way for members of the general public to view the Peercoin blockchain, web developers have created block explorers. They present different layouts, statistics and charts. Block explorers allow the following information to be discovered:

- **Height of block**   —the block number of the network.

- **Time of block**   —the time at which the block was timestamped to the blockchain.

- **Transactions**   —the number of transactions in that particular block.

- **Total Sent**   —the total amount of cryptocurrency sent in that particular block.

- **Block Reward**   —how many coins were generated by the block (added to the overall coin circulation).

All recognised Peercoin block explorers can be found on the official Peercoin website at https://peercoin.net/resources.html#blockexplorers

What follows is block number 1 of the Peercoin blockchain:

Details for Block #1

Hash	00000000000be4e024af5071ba515c7510767f42ec9e40c5fba56775ff296658 >
Date/Time	2012-08-19 18:19:16
Transactions	1
Value Out	2,499.75 PPC
Difficulty	256
Outstanding	2,499.75 PPC
Created	2,499.75 PPC

PROOF OF STAKE

As an alternative to the proof of work timestamping algorithm used for securing the Bitcoin network protocol, Sunny King and Scott Nadal invented proof of stake in 2012 to secure Peercoin. It relies on minters (Peercoin wallet users holding PPC) to produce new blocks. Instead of using vast amounts of electricity, time is used as the limited resource to automatically and randomly select the minter who produces the next block. A minter who accumulates a high "coin age" (defined below), has a higher probability of minting the next block.

> "Coin age is a number that is derived from multiplying the amount of coins a minter owns by the number of days those coins have been held in their wallet. A minter who has high coin age for example has both a high number of coins in their wallet and those coins have also been sitting in that wallet for quite a long period of time."

To prevent minters with high "coin age" from being able to hold a monopoly on the block generation process and to give others a better chance of minting, a few protocol code rules exist:

- Minters must hold the coins for at least 30 days before being eligible to mint.

- After participating coins from a minter have been used to mint a new block, their "coinage" is reset back to zero.

- A minter's probability of finding a new block reaches its maximum after 90 days. After this period of time, a minter's stake reaches maturity and their chances of minting a new block are maxed out

On the 18th September 2012, the first ever proof of stake block was timestamped to the Peercoin blockchain:

Block #6,325 (Reward 1.98 PPC) September 18th 2012 at 22:01:24 UTC

ECONOMICS OF PEERCOIN

Unlike Bitcoin, the Peercoin blockchain has no fixed coin supply limit. Wallet users receive about 1% annual interest on held PPC by participating in the minting process. However, due to the generation of proof of work blocks, the supply increases by more than 1% per year (see table below).

Date	Block	Total PPC Generated	Inflation p.a.
19th August 2014	128,270	21,651,260	8.12%
19th August 2015	196,039	22,637,929	4.56%
19th August 2016	253,728	23,432,611	3.51%
19th August 2017	318,210	24,273,167	3.59%
19th August 2018	382,333	24,917,534	2.65%

Being the world's first hybrid blockchain, utilising both proof of stake and proof of work, Peercoin draws strength from both consensus mechanisms:

- Proof of work timestamping provides the network with the majority of newly generated coins (distribution). Each proof of work block reward is inversely proportional to the hash power committed by miners to find it.

- Proof of stake timestamping is used to mint the majority of new blocks and is the way in which decentralisation is sustained (security). It is more energy efficient, because it uses time, not electricity, as the scarce resource.

Besides coin generation, there is a deflationary aspect that helps to reduce the rate at which the size of the Peercoin blockchain grows. When wallet client users send PPC, they must pay a transaction fee (0.01 PPC per kb). These fees are permanently removed from the circulating supply.

QUICK GUIDE FOR INVESTORS

What follows is a quick guide for investors put together by Peercoin enthusiast and active community member Ötzi:

Q: WILL PEERCOIN STILL BE AROUND 50 YEARS FROM NOW?
A: Yes. The combination of Proof of stake and Proof of work provides perfect economic incentives for all participants to keep the blockchain alive and secure.

Q: INFLATION
A: Expect between 250.000 and 500.000 new coins to be created per year. Not much compared to the 25.000.000 coins in existence, but a significant amount in the long run. The exact height of inflation depends on a number of different factors, you can research them yourself.

Q: GETTING STARTED
A: Buy the coins, download the client, and send them to the address provided by the client.

Q: DO I NEED TO SET UP A STAKING NODE?
A: No. The 1% annual reward is minimal, and the Peercoin system does not require all investors to stake. It's ok if you just store your coins. Others will secure the blockchain for you. Change your mind later, and you will still get a reward.

Q: I WANT TO STAKE MY COINS. WHAT DO I NEED?
A: The probability to mint a block and get a reward is higher the more coins you have. With 100 coins, you need to stay online 24/7 to have a very good chance to mint a block at least once per year. A Stakebox is ideal for that, because it consumes very little energy. Once you own 3.000 coins or more, staking becomes easy. This amount of coins will stake very fast, so you can just open your wallet once every 3 months and mint a block within a few days. But if you own less than 100 coins, forget about staking.

Q: WANT TO BECOME AN EXPERT?
A: Go to the Peercoin-Github, read up the build-info in the "doc"-folder, and then compile the client yourself. Or, build and sign raw transactions in the debug-console.

PEERCOIN FOUNDATION

For several years, prominent members of the Peercoin team rejected the idea of forming a foundation due to it being considered as a form of centralisation. On the 14th May 2018, the team established the Peercoin Foundation. It was registered in Amsterdam, The Netherlands.

> "The governments of the world are watching crypto more than ever. Exchanges require the signing of NDAs in order to apply for listings. With the rise of ICOs and the rampant commercialisation of all things blockchain, coders who once volunteered their time for free to project they believe in have been replaced by paid work."

The Peercoin Foundation makes it possible for the project to legally collect donations from the community for funding continued development, marketing and other operational activities. Developers will be sufficiently paid to enhance the Peercoin blockchain. Two multi-signature donation wallet addresses exist on the Peercoin website at https://peercoin.net/foundation.html

CRYPTOCURRENCY EXCHANGES

Besides acquiring PPC via staking or mining, they can be bought and sold using cryptocurrency exchanges. Some exchanges require users to fully register by submitting certain documentation including proof of identity and address. On the other hand, most exchanges only require users to register by creating a simple username and password with the use of an e-mail account.

At the time this book was published, the top 3 Peercoin trading exchanges were:

What follows below, and on the adjacent page, is a list of all known exchanges that have initiated PPC trading:

Date Trading Initiated	Exchange	Trading Against	Status
4th September 2012	Cryptocoin		CLOSED
7th September 2012	Bitparking		CLOSED
18th November 2012	Vircurex	BTC	CLOSED
6th April 2013	BTC-e	BTC, USD	CLOSED
24th April 2013	Bter	BTC, LTC, CNY	CLOSED
23rd May 2013	Cryptsy	BTC, LTC, USD	CLOSED
28th May 2013	Crypto Trade	BTC, USD	CLOSED
22nd June 2013	Coins-e	BTC	CLOSED

CRYPTOCURRENCY EXCHANGES

Date Trading Initiated	Exchange	Trading Against	Status
19th September 2013	mcxNOW	BTC	CLOSED
30th September 2013	CoinEX	BTC	CLOSED
28th October 2013	Vault of Satoshi		CLOSED
29th January 2014	Bittylicious	GBP	ACTIVE
13th February 2014	Bittrex	BTC	ACTIVE
8th April 2014	Poloniex	BTC	ACTIVE
22nd April 2014	The Rock Trading	BTC, EUR	ACTIVE
13th May 2014	Coinnext	BTC	CLOSED
18th June 2014	CCEDK	BTC	CLOSED
6th December 2014	Cryptopia	BTC, LTC, DOGE	ACTIVE
5th January 2015	Yobit	BTC	ACTIVE
6th April 2016	LiteBit.eu	EUR	ACTIVE
14th June 2016	Southxchange	BTC	ACTIVE
17th August 2017	HitBTC	BTC, USD	ACTIVE
20th October 2017	Bitsane	BTC	ACTIVE
29th November 2017	Tux Exchange	BTC	ACTIVE
22nd December 2017	Livecoin	BTC	ACTIVE
14th September 2018	Kompler	BTC, ETH	ACTIVE
17th September 2018	Coin Switch		ACTIVE
8th January 2019	BitTurk	TRY	ACTIVE
15th January 2019	Amsterdex	BTC	ACTIVE
20th February 2019	BC Bitcoin		ACTIVE

WALLETS

A wallet is basically a piece of software that can be used on a personal computer, tablet or smartphone. It allows users to store PPC as well as execute transfers of the coins with other users. Alternatively, it can be described as a means to access the coins from the inseparable blockchain (public distributed ledger). The software can be accessed, downloaded and installed from the official Peercoin website at https://peercoin.net/wallet.html

What follows is a list of the different types of Peercoin wallet:

- Desktop wallet client for Windows, Mac O SX and Linux. It enables users to participate in the minting process, and hence securing the network.

- Modern paper wallet generator.

- Unofficial wallets provided by third parties.

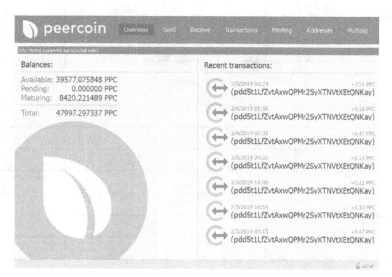

COMMUNITY

A community is a social unit or network that shares common values, goals and dreams. Peercoin has a community consisting of an innumerable number of people who have the coin's wellbeing and future success at heart. The majority of these people prefer fictitious names with optional avatars. Prominent members of the community (the Peercoin team) include Sunny King, Sentinelrv, Peerchemist, Backpacker, Sigmike, Buckkets, Hrobeers, Nagalim and Saeveritt.

There are different social media platforms on which the community discuss ideas and post announcements related to Peercoin. There are also official websites on which people can read informative material. What follows are some of the important websites related to the project:

- Bitcointalk: https://bitcointalk.org/index.php?topic=101820.0

- Discord: https://discord.gg/XPxfwtG

- Facebook: https://www.facebook.com/Peercoin/

- Official Forum: https://talk.peercoin.net/

- Reddit: https://www.reddit.com/r/peercoin/

- Telegram: https://t.me/peercoin

- Twitter: https://twitter.com/PeercoinPPC

- YouTube: https://www.youtube.com/user/PeerCoin

In essence, the community surrounding and participating in the development of Peercoin is the backbone of the blockchain. Without a following, the prospects of future adoption and utilisation are starkly limited. Peercoin belongs to all those who use it, not just to the developers who aid its progression.

x

A CONCISE HISTORY OF PEERCOIN

CHAPTERS

I.   PPCOIN ANNOUNCED ON 10TH AUGUST 2012

II.   PPCOIN BLOCKCHAIN LAUNCHED ON 19TH AUGUST 2012

III.   CRYPTOCOIN, BITPARKING AND VIRCUREX INITIATED PPC TRADING

IV.   PPCOIN SWITCHED TO VERSION 0.2 ON 10TH SEPTEMBER 2012

V.   FIRST PPC POS BLOCK TIMESTAMPED ON 18TH SEPTEMBER 2012

1

LAUNCH OF THE
PPCOIN BLOCKCHAIN

"The PPCoin blockchain launched on the 19th August 2012."

After ten months of research and discovery, Sunny King announced PPCoin (the original name of Peercoin) to the wider cryptocurrency community via the online forum Bitcointalk. He created a pre-release thread on that forum titled "[ANN] [PPC] PPCoin Beta Release Soon" on the 10th August 2012 at 14:18:31 UTC in anticipation of a future launch of the PPCoin blockchain. Sunny King posted:

> **"I am happy to announce that project ppcoin is now close to beta quality
> and will be released to public soon."**

On the 16th August 2012, Sunny King notified the fledging PPCoin community that the first PPC release build of the core qt wallet client was being prepared. He stated a tentative blockchain launch time had been set for the 19th August 2012 at 18:00 UTC.

Sunny King emphasised the experimental nature of the initial PPC release build, and recommended that potential users of the software carry out their own security evaluations. He promised to make it as secure as possible and praised the community for their support so far.

On the 16th August 2012 at 23:31 BST, PPC version 0.1.0 was released and made accessible via the PPCoin Github repository website. Download links were also created on the original PPCoin website www.ppcoin.org (see image below) and on the official pre-release PPCoin Bitcointalk thread. Users were given ample time to install the software and prepare their mining rigs before launch in two to three days time.

On the following day, FuzzyBear posted his first comment on the official PPCoin pre-release Bitcointalk thread:

> "I will be there on sunday to support you with your coin :) best of luck and
> hope the release goes ahead!! Will u be releasing a wallet and miner??"

On the 19th August 2012, approximately twelve hours before the scheduled launch of the PPCoin blockchain, Sunny King published the PPCoin Design Paper. Members of the community, keen to read and investigate the technicalities of the coin, were able to gain access to it via the official website. As shown below, the original PPCoin website (created by Sunny King) was a single page featuring five icons. From left to right, these were the design paper, the source code, the client download, the PPC wiki and chat forum (PPCoin Bitcointalk thread).

2012-2013 PPCoin Developers

Block #1 (Reward 2,499.75 PPC) August 19th 2012 at 18:19:16 UTC

On the 19th August 2012, the PPCoin blockchain launched. The first block (see above) was timestamped at 18:19:16 UTC via proof of work mining.

One hour later, Sunny King created a new PPCoin Bitcointalk thread. It was titled "[ANN] [PPC] PPCoin Released! - First Long-Term Energy-Efficient Crypto-Currency" and became the thread on which to discuss PPCoin related material.

On the 26th August 2012, Sunny King posted his first weekly update:

> "PPCoin has sailed through our first week without a problem. There is a small annoyance where users see quite a bit exception messages in debug log about tx messages, and is linked to Bitcoin transactions somehow broadcasted on our network. We are currently investigating a network protocol upgrade for v0.2 to solve this problem. Blockchain and user transactions have been working normally throughout the week and not affected by this annoyance.
>
> In v0.2 a main chain protocol upgrade is expected as I described in [Bitcointalk thread]. The code of this has been done, as well as some other improvements. This protocol switch is important and will help us achieve the goal of decentralisation in the future. I am also working on setting up public test network. Over next week v0.2 code would go through testing and be prepared for release.
>
> I didn't expect that within the first week both a mining pool (NothinG) and a forum website (FuzzyBear) were set up with the ppcoin network. Kudos to our ardent and productive supporters and I believe our still small community has great prospects.
>
> While the proof-of-stake blocks are still not due for another 3 weeks, our users should have already observed our difficulty adjustment is continuous. In principle it isn't that much different from Bitcoin, standard averaging techniques are used to achieve constant adjustment. This design helped a lot during our first 3 days, where difficulty climbed from an initial 256 to over 3000. The constant adjustment of difficulty also helps with protecting the kernel, but this is probably a bit premature to be discussed right now.
>
> First week total mintage is 3~4 million coins. We thank our supporters for contributing resources to help the network get started. I am an entrepreneurial type as well as an architect/techie, and I understand taking risks deserves matching reward. The mint curve is quite fair in my opinion, as everyone has free choice to participate in the early stages.
>
> Have fun and next week!"

On the 31st August 2012, PPC version 0.2.0 was released. It was a mandatory requirement for users to upgrade to this version before the 10th September 2012, or otherwise find themselves disconnected from the main PPCoin blockchain network protocol. Besides improving the client software, it introduced:

> "In the new release there are some minor improvements for
> getblock and getinfo. You can now see the total network money supply
> via getinfo. For getblock you can now see the mint amount for the block, as
> well as an additional option to see details of all transactions in the block."

On the 4th September 2012, the first cryptocurrency exchange initiated PPC trading. Bitcointalk user "mugen" was pleased to announce that Cryptocoin had gone live. Both Sunny King and FuzzyBear praised its opening:

> Sunny King: "Congratulations to mugen and Cryptocoin Exchange
> being the first to start trading ppcoin :)"
>
> FuzzyBear: "Gratz mugen and Cryptocoin Exchange… u beat me to it!!"

Three days later, the second exchange to initiate PPC trading went live. Bitcointalk user "doublec" had created Bitparking. Bitparking registered over 200,000 PPC trading volume on its first day. It closed in April 2013.

On the 10th September 2012, the PPCoin blockchain network switched to version 0.2.0 at 18:00 UTC. Also on this day, the value of 1 PPC was recorded at approximately 0.00015 BTC.

An important milestone occurred on the 18th September 2012. The first proof of stake block was timestamped to the PPCoin blockchain (below).

Block #6,325 (Reward 1.98 PPC) September 18th 2012 at 22:01:24 UTC

Also on the 18th September 2012, PPC version 0.2.1 was released. It included a code bug fix related to the 'checkwallet' wallet command. Other minor code fixes were also made. It was not a mandatory upgrade.

On the 30th September 2012, Sunny King announced that work had begun on PPC version 0.3 code development. He also pointed out that the proportion of proof of stake blocks to the overall number of blocks, being timestamped to the PPCoin blockchain, had been increasing. Proof of stake blocks were approaching the set ten minute block spacing target.

Since the 26th August 2012, Sunny King had been posting weekly updates on the official PPCoin Bitcointalk thread. On the 2nd October 2012, due to popular request from the PPCoin community, he started to post his updates on a separate Bitcointalk thread with links to the main thread. The community wanted Sunny King to keep all updates separate from the PPCoin Bitcointalk discussion. The first six Sunny King weekly updates were:

Weekly Update #1 on 26th August 2012 16:14:04 UTC
Weekly Update #2 on 2nd September 2012 17:51:51 UTC
Weekly Update #3 on 9th September 2012 17:29:27 UTC
Weekly Update #4 on 16th September 2012 at 22:25:43 UTC
Weekly Update #5 on 24th September 2012 at 01:26:29 UTC
Weekly Update #6 on 30th September 2012 at 17:27:26 UTC

On the 3rd October 2012, the total number of PPC generated via both proof of work and stake surpassed 10,000,000 at the following block:

Block #8,186 (Reward 1,010.45 PPC) October 3rd 2012 at 00:50:42 UTC

Other events which occurred during October 2012 were:

- Sunny King reported that he was making good progress with PPC version 0.3.0, but that its release would be delayed due to his heavy workload during the last two months of the year.

- Satoshi Roulette was the first non-exchange website to accept PPC as a form of payment.

- On the 15th October 2012, block number 10,000 was timestamped to the PPCoin blockchain at 10:41:39 UTC via proof of stake timestamping.

During the first few days of November 2012, over half of all blocks timestamping to the PPCoin blockchain were proof of stake.

On the 11th November 2012, PPC version 0.2.2 was released. It fixed issues with the money supply statistics being displayed and 'coinstake' creation. Improvements were also made to the core qt graphical user interface (GUI) to make it easier for users to see their staked coin total and staked transactions.

Two months after the first two cryptocurrency exchanges included PPC trading, a third exchange Vircurex (short for Virtual Currency Exchange) began to offer its users the ability to buy/sell PPC on the 18th November 2012.

Vircurex was founded in October 2011 and subsequently went live on the 22nd October 2011. It suddenly closed down a couple of years later.

On the 28th November 2012, the proof of work mining block reward of the Bitcoin blockchain halved from 50 BTC to 25 BTC. As shown below, block number 210,000 was the first block of the Bitcoin blockchain to generate 25 BTC.

As a consequence, the difficulty of mining PPC proof of work blocks substantially increased. This was due to the fact that Bitcoin miners found themselves in the position of receiving only half the profits. Bitcoin miners were then attracted to more profitable cryptocurrencies, PPCoin being one of only a few coins at the time. Sunny King cautioned the PPCoin community about potential PPC price volatility.

Block #209,999 (Reward 50 BTC) November 28th 2012 at 15:01:40 UTC

Block #210,000 (Reward 25 BTC) November 28th 2012 at 15:24:38 UTC

> **Block #21,841 (Reward 728.41 PPC) December 26th 2012 at 22:45:34 UTC**

On the 26th December 2012, the total number of PPC generated to date surpassed 15,000,000 at block number 21,841 (see above).

On the 31st December 2012, Sunny King reported that PPC version 0.3.0 was undergoing code development. He emphasised his commitment to uphold the security and proper functionality of the PPCoin blockchain. He also wished the whole PPCoin community a happy new year.

On the topic of PPC trading, the cryptocurrency exchange Vircurex recorded a closing value of 33,100 Bitcoin Satoshi (1 Bitcoin Satoshi = 0.00000001 BTC) on the 31st December 2012.

Other events which occurred during this period included:

- On the 26th August 2012, the first official PPCoin forum opened for registrations at www.ppcointalk.org where the community could better discuss PPCoin related material. FuzzyBear encouraged registered users to leave feedback on its design, functionality and ease of navigation.

- On the 26th August 2012, the first PPCoin subreddit was created at www.reddit.com/r/ppcoin at 22:51:11 UTC.

- On the 2nd September 2012, the total number of PPC surpassed 5 million.

- On the 11th September 2012, the Bitparking mining pool went live.

- On the 18th September 2012, Bitcointalk user "dreamwatcher" announced the first PPCoin block explorer at https://www.ppcexplore.org:2750/ had been launched. One day later, it changed to www.ppcexplore.org

- On the 19th November 2012, Bitcointalk user "xchrix" launched a website at www.cryptocoincharts.info showing many crypto price chart statistics.

- On the 3rd December 2012, Bitcointalk user "xchrix" launched the first website at www.cryptocoinsend.com to support PPC processing payments.

I.   PPCOIN VERSION 0.3.0 CODE DEVELOPMENT CONTINUED

II.   FIRST PPCOIN FORKED COIN LAUNCHED ON 9TH FEBRUARY 2013

III.   PPCOIN VERSION 0.3.0 WAS RELEASED ON 16TH FEBRUARY 2013

IV.   BTC-E EXCHANGE INITIATED PPC TRADING ON 6TH APRIL 2013

V.   PPCOIN ADDED TO COINMARKETCAP.COM ON 28TH APRIL 2013

2

PPCOIN SWITCHED TO VERSION 0.3 PROTOCOL

"The transition for users should have minimal impact as
there is no effect on existing wallet balance, transactions and minting
related protocols of the network." - Sunny King

Sunny King, and the PPCoin community as a whole, were pleased about how well the first several months had proceeded. There was great optimism as PPCoin development entered 2013.

During the first week of January 2013, Sunny King announced that the code for the future PPC version 0.3.0 release was 80% complete. He emphasised the need for further preliminary code testing and at least two more weeks to meticulously check it. It was important to not rush, so as to avoid potential flaws that would otherwise arise. He anticipated release by the end of the month.

On the 1st January 2013, the first block of the year was timestamped to the PPCoin blockchain at block number 22,707 via proof of stake timestamping (see below).

Block #22,707 (Reward 0.64 PPC) January 1st 2013 at 00:11:48 UTC

On the 15th January 2013, Sunny King announced that PPC version 0.3.0 had reached 90% code completion. The first round of code testing had been successful.

On the 21st January 2013, code testing revealed some bugs. Sunny King posted:

> "The 0.3 protocol upgrade involves changing the way hash is computed to generate stake transactions (known as coinstake). The transition for users should have minimal impact as there is no effect on existing wallet balance, transactions and minting related protocols of the network. The new protocol replaces the current proof-of-stake difficulty in the role of *stake modifier* inside the proof-of-stake hashing computation (not to be confused with proof-of-work hashing, which remains unchanged)."

On the 28th January 2013, PPC version 0.3.0 protocol code was complete. It was then crucial to thoroughly test it before release.

On the 9th February 2013, the first fork of the PPCoin blockchain Novacoin launched. Sunny King stated that he had not been involved in creating or launching the Novacoin (NVC) blockchain, but was happy to see other developers valuing the PPCoin code design. He was quoted as saying:

> "Well congratulations to the first running ppcoin fork ;) Okay I am a bit surprised but happy :D I think forks are endorsements of the value of our work and I don't mind more competition" :D

NOVACOIN INITIAL SPECIFICATION SUMMARY

Blockchain launched:	9th February 2013 at 16:21:22 UTC
Symbol:	NVC
Founder:	Balthazar
Hashing Algorithm:	Scrypt
Timestamping Algorithm:	Proof of Work/Proof of Stake

After weeks of code testing on testnet had found no significant issues, PPC version 0.3.0 (based on Bitcoin version 0.6.3) was released on the 16th February 2013. It included the stake generation protocol upgrade. Users had to upgrade before the scheduled 20th March 2013 protocol switch date.

On the 23rd February 2013, Sunny King was quoted as saying:

> "A good couple of months for me. I am relieved that 0.3 is finally done. And I also enjoy watching all the new projects going on like ripple and novacoin."

On the 19th March 2013, FuzzyBear was pleased to announce the launch of the revamped and improved PPCoin community chat forum. It was an opportunity for members of the community to have more managed, organised and professional discussions related to PPCoin. FuzzyBear posted the following post:

> "Hey all finally got a better forum for PPCoin sorted out :) most should all be more familiar with this. Feel free to sign up, I will be moving the URL to http://www.ppcointalk.org but that will not change the users created on here http://new.ppcointalk.org
>
> I will leave the old site up until I move the content across, sorry but I don't think it will be possible to port the user accounts across.
>
> Let me know of any bugs or suggestions and have fun with your PPCoins!"

On the following day, the PPCoin blockchain successfully switched to the version 0.3.0 protocol code.

On the 6th April 2013, BTC-e (www.btc-e.com) became the fourth cryptocurrency exchange to initiate PPC trading. A single PPC/BTC trading pair went live. A total of 631,271 PPC were traded on the exchange on the first day.

BTC-e, which launched on the 7th August 2011, was operational until the US government seized their website domain address in July 2017.

During the first week of April 2013, the PPCoin market capitalisation surged. It attained a value over US$8,000,000 on the 9th April 2013, and Sunny King posted the following on the official PPCoin Bitcointalk thread:

> "What a week! PPCoin has achieved multiple milestones in the cryptocurrency market this week. Market cap surpassed namecoin and now ranked behind litecoin at 50,000 BTC or over $8M as of today, or about 0.5% of bitcoin and over 10% of litecoin."

On the 22nd April 2013, Sunny King posted his first official statement on the PPCoin chat forum at www.ppcointalk.org and welcomed all registered users there:

> "First I'd like to thank FuzzyBear for his hard work of hosting this nice forum. As you know that bitcointalk's altcoin forum is getting very crowded these days with different altcoins it becomes more and more difficult to follow ppcoin threads there. So as we gain more popularity I will begin to visit this forum more often.

> As you probably already know, that we are among the very few cryptocurrency projects that actually attempt at real innovations, rather than just cloning bitcoin and making some small tweaks. I believe the future of cryptocurrency to be a very competitive market, with multiple major currencies of different designs. We are still a fairly young project, most people still don't know about our innovations and cannot distinguish us from all the clone altcoins. This is where our supporters can join forces and help the community grow, by raising awareness in the cryptocurrency market about the benefit of continued innovation in this field and the need to support real innovations.

> I would like to also thank our supporters for your personal encouragements to me, it means a lot to me. We must remember what the cryptocurrency movement represents to humanity, a return of monetary power back to the free market, an upgraded guard of private property, one of the pillars of human civilization. Armed with this new advancement, liberty now has a better chance. I am so happy there are people out there sharing the same view with me, so that I know I am not alone walking the path, and together we will gain more courage, help each other, and make the history."

On the 28th April 2013, a ranking service at www.coinmarketcap.com went live with seven cryptocurrencies: Bitcoin, Litecoin, Peercoin, Namecoin, Terracoin, Devcoin and Novacoin. It has since grown to rank over two thousand cryptocurrencies (coins and tokens).

What follows is a table derived from www.coinmarketcap.com showing the first two days of recorded historical figures related to PPCoin:

	Low US$	Open US$	Close US$	High US$	Market Cap US$
28th April 2013	0.376287	0.386958	0.386525	0.404659	7,250,189
29th April 2013	0.377908	0.387200	0.408861	0.424765	7,673,915

Sunny King was happy to witness the growing PPCoin community. There were more people showing an interest in, or contributing to, the development of the project. He reiterated the goal of PPCoin as being to achieve energy efficient operation in the long term. He was also looking forward to beginning work on PPC version 0.4 and other improvements.

Other events which occurred during this period included:

- On the 4th March 2013, the first official PPCoin Facebook page was created at the www.facebook.com/PPcoin domain address.

- On the 22nd April 2013, DirectVoltage.com was the first retailer to accept PPC as a form of payment on their website.

- On the 24th April 2013, a Chinese based cryptocurrency exchange called Bter initiated the PPC/BTC, PPC/LTC and PPC/CNY trading pairs.

I.   PPCOIN BECAME KNOWN AS PEERCOIN IN MAY 2013

II.   CRYPTSY EXCHANGE INITIATED PPC TRADING ON 23RD MAY 2013

III.   PRIMECOIN BLOCKCHAIN LAUNCHED ON 7TH JULY 2013

IV.   NEW PEERCOIN LOGO ADOPTED ON 13TH JULY 2013

V.   VITALIK BUTERIN INTERVIEWED SUNNY KING ON 8TH AUGUST 2013

3

NEW PEERCOIN LOGO
DESIGN CHOSEN

*"Many thanks to Sentinelrv for again all your hard work in keeping
this vote / contest running... would not have happened without you."* - FuzzyBear

A change from the original name PPCoin to Peercoin began to gain momentum in late April 2013. Some members of the community also saw the name change as an opportunity to propose a new PPC logo. In particular, two Bitcointalk users called "robotrebellion" (below, left) and "mjbmonetarymetals" (below, right) proposed designs. Sunny King posted the following response:

**"Thanks to robotrebellion and mjbmonetarymetals for contribution
of graphic work. Oh and a new term 'eco-friendly'."**

On the 3rd May 2013, Sentinelrv posted his first comment on the official PPCoin chat forum. He said:

> "I've been waiting since last night to post this, since I was relegated to the newbie forum, but I love the new logo, if that is indeed what we're sticking with. I made it my new avatar. I think it helps bring Peercoin a little more credibility. I just wish the website was updated now to be more friendly and informative to new people."

Sunny King supported community participation in designing a new PPCoin logo, but wanted to keep the P symbol (the official symbol at this time was two P's connected by a bar). On the 6th May 2013, more coin logo designs were publicly posted by detail3, including the following:

On the 8th May 2013, Bitcointalk user "mjbmonetarymetals" created another design (see below). Sentinelrv slightly altered the design by making the symbol look more like PP, instead of IP.

During May 2013, three more forks of the PPCoin blockchain were launched. Once again, Sunny King welcomed these, reiterating that an increasing number of developers were valuing the PPCoin protocol code. These forks were:

- On the 2nd May 2013, the second PPC fork BitBar (left) launched.

- On the 8th May 2013, the third PPC fork YACoin (centre) launched.

- On the 16th May 2013, the fourth PPC fork Bitgem (right) launched.

In recognition of the name change from PPCoin to Peercoin, the location of the PPC chat forum moved from www.ppcointalk.org to www.peercointalk.org on the 21st May 2013.

On the 23rd May 2013, three days after the exchange launched, Cryptsy initiated PPC trading. It was a cryptocurrency exchange based in Delray Beach, Florida, USA.

Cryptsy®

On the 6th June 2013, Sentinelrv made an announcement detailing how the community would choose the new PPC logo. An online website called 99Designs had been chosen. Initially, the 'gold package' (~US$800) was picked to give Peercoin the greatest exposure of submissions and a future poll to choose the best design. Also, a gofundme.com account had been created to help raise funds.

Sentinelrv was clear that, at the end of the logo design contest, work would begin on professionally redesigning the official Peercoin website. He knew it would help to optimise the marketing of the coin to a wider audience.

On the following day, Sentinelrv created a www.peercointalk.org thread titled "Peercoin Logo Design Contest Fundraising Thread". Members of the community were encouraged to spread awareness of the contest via social media.

New Peercoin Logo Design Chosen

On the 13th June 2013, Sentinelrv chose to downgrade to the 99Designs 'Bronze package'. It was considered sufficient to achieve required goals. Thanks to forum user "whifmoi", the total US$300 was raised on this day. FuzzyBear said:

> "Nice work here everyone especially Sentinelrv and serious congratulations on raising the funding. Let's keep the ball rolling, so what is the next stage? Maybe you want to outline this in the OP or a new thread... feel free to make a sticky thread or ask me or an admin to do this if you cannot."

After giving the community ample time to draw up designs, Sentinelrv announced the 99Designs "Peercoin Logo Design Contest" as live on the 27th June 2013. As much feedback as possible was welcomed in order for the final design to be the most attractive and appealing image of the coin.

On the 28th June 2013, Sunny King announced another cryptocurrency he had been working on:

> "I am happy to launch another innovative cryptocurrency design soon. Primecoin project was under development since March. It was meant to complement ppcoin in our technology portfolio. Primecoin introduces the first non-hashcash proof-of-work, prime number proof-of-work, the first proof-of-work in cryptocurrency that not only provides minting and security, but also provides additional potential scientific values. This advancement will pave the way for future proof-of-work types with diverse scientific values and uses.

> Primecoin is currently tentatively scheduled to be released next week (July 7th). Please visit the pre-release thread for updates.

> Primecoin network would complement ppcoin network to strengthen our strategic position in the highly competitive cryptocurrency market."

At the beginning of July 2013, the logo design contest was the predominant topic of conversation. At the end of the contest, 40 designers had submitted a total of 217 designs between them.

On the 2nd July 2013, the qualifying voting round began. Members of the community had the chance to vote for their favourite six designers. After two days, Lightning received the most votes (15), and LesDeane was second with nine votes.

What follows are some of the most popular designs submitted during the contest:

#109 by Lightning

#197 by LesDeaneGraphics

#91 by GameKyuubi

#178 by Miroslav22

#156 by PhatCowDesigns

#48 by Lightning

#175 by Akaki

#35 by Lightning

On the 7th July 2013, the Primecoin blockchain launched at 18:28:00 UTC. The Greek letter psi was chosen to represent the coin's currency symbol (see logo, below, right) as tribute to Riemann.

On the 13th July 2013, after two days of a final voting round, the winner of the "Peercoin Logo Design Contest" was unveiled. Lightning was the winner and his design was accepted as the visual representation (see below, left) of Peercoin from this day forward. Sunny King congratulated Sentinelrv for organising the contest and loved the new Peercoin logo.

FuzzyBear also praised Sentinelrv and the entire community for their participation in the contest. He posted the following:

> "Many thanks to Sentinelrv for again all your hard work in keeping this vote / contest running... would not have happened without you so the community owes you... except for the developers who will now have to make all new builds and website icons and logos!! But seriously thank you from everyone over at http://www.peercointalk.org as well."

On the 16th August 2013, the total number of PPC generated to date surpassed 20,000,000 as soon as the block below was timestamped to the Peercoin blockchain. Block number 64,260 was timestamped via proof of stake.

Block #64,260 (Reward 43.66 PPC) August 16th 2013 at 08:47:09 UTC

Other events which occurred during this period included:

- On the 2nd May 2013, a new subreddit at .../r/peercoin was created.

- On the 22nd May 2013, PPC tipping went live on Reddit.

- On the 28th May 2013, the Crypto Trade exchange initiated PPC trading.

- On the 2nd June 2013, Jason Schaumleffel uploaded a video to YouTube detailing the characteristics of Peercoin.

- On the 22nd June 2013, the Coins-e exchange initiated PPC trading. It was on the opening day of the exchange as PPC trading went live beside fifteen other cryptocurrencies.

- On the 23rd June 2013, the fifth PPC fork Bottlecaps launched.

- On the 27th June 2013, the sixth PPC fork Crypto Bullion launched.

- On the 8th August 2013, Sunny King was interviewed by Vitalik Buterin as part of an article for Bitcoin Magazine. It lasted for two hours and twenty minutes. The full transcript of the interview can be read in the appendix of this book from page 138 to page 148.

I.   PEERCOIN FIRST YEAR ANNIVERSARY ON 19TH AUGUST 2013

II.   JORDAN LEE INTRODUCED PEERSHARES IN SEPTEMBER 2013

III.   PEERCOIN MARKET CAPITALISATION SURPASSED US$10,000,000

IV.   TWO PEERCOINTALK COMMUNITY INTERVIEWS WITH SUNNY KING

V.   VAULT OF SATOSHI ADDED PPC TRADING ON 28TH OCTOBER 2013

4

COMMUNITY GROWTH
AND PARTICIPATION

"The official Peercoin website will act as an information hub that will contribute to many people's understanding of what makes Peercoin better than Bitcoin. That awareness of the benefits of Peercoin is what we want." - Sentinelrv

Besides great community satisfaction about the new Peercoin logo, there were frequent posts on the Peercoin forum. Many threads were being created for the community to discuss a wide span of topics related to code development, social awareness campaigns and other issues. Peercointalk user JustaBitofTime (left the community in late 2013) was highly active in campaigns directed at increasing Peercoin adoption. Other notable team players included Sentinelrv, FuzzyBear, Super3, Irritant and, of course, Sunny King.

On the 19th August 2013, the community celebrated the first year anniversary of the coin. The Peercoin blockchain turned one year old as soon as block number 64,853 was timestamped via proof of stake (see below).

Block #64,853 (Reward 0.14 PPC) August 19th 2013 at 18:22:30 UTC

On the 26th August 2013, Vitalik Buterin published an article titled "What Proof of Stake Is And Why It Matters" for Bitcoin Magazine. He had already interviewed Sunny King (pages 138-148) eighteen days earlier. What follows is the first paragraph of the article related to proof of stake:

> "However, there is one SHA256 alternative that is already here, and that essentially does away with the computational waste of proof of work entirely: proof of stake. Rather than requiring the prover to perform a certain amount of computational work, a proof of stake system requires the prover to show ownership of a certain amount of money. The reason why Satoshi could not have done this himself is simple: before 2009, there was no kind of digital property which could securely interact with cryptographic protocols. Paypal and online credit card payments have been around for over ten years, but those systems are centralized, so creating a proof of stake system around them would allow Paypal and credit card providers themselves to cheat it by generating fake transactions. IP addresses and domain names are partially decentralised, but there is no way to construct a proof of ownership of either that could be verified in the future. Indeed, the first digital property that could possibly work with an online proof of stake system is Bitcoin (and cryptocurrency in general) itself."

As a way for businesses to manage publicly held shares in a decentralised manner, Jordan Lee introduced a Peercoin related project on the 28th September 2013. He called it Peershares. He envisaged leveraging Peercoin, and proof of stake timestamping, to accomplish it.

Going forward, Jordan Lee wanted to develop, and then launch, a separate blockchain based only on proof of stake. He also had plans to create an alternative, feature rich version of the PPC core qt wallet client (later known as Peerunity). He stressed it would not require changes to the Peercoin blockchain protocol code and he was ready to do most of the work himself.

During September 2013, two cryptocurrency exchanges initiated PPC trading:

- On the 19th September 2013, mcxNOW initiated the PPC/BTC trading pair. The exchange is no longer operational.

- On the 30th September 2013, CoinEX initiated the PPC/BTC trading pair at https://coinex.pw/trade/ppc_btc and launched its own built-in mining pool.

During the early UTC hours on the 5th October 2013, the PPC market capitalisation surpassed US$10,000,000 for the first time, but only momentarily. Sunny King, in one of his weekly updates, was quoted as saying:

"PPC briefly touched $10 million cap, consolidating the lead over NMC as the 3rd in market cap behind BTC and LTC. Trading volume has been impressive last few days. PPC proof-of-work difficulty breaks 6 million and block reward drops under 200. The current annual inflation rate of PPC is approaching that of BTC."

What follows is a table of historical figures derived from www.coinmarketcap.com that shows the ascent in both the US Dollar price of 1 PPC and the overall PPC market capitalisation leading up to the US$10,000,000 milestone:

	Low US$	Open US$	Close US$	High US$	Market Cap US$
3rd October 2013	0.266132	0.284981	0.294239	0.308103	6,026,298
4th October 2013	0.293183	0.293716	0.439924	0.451780	9,012,444
5th October 2013	0.386517	0.436056	0.496203	0.552852	10,171,962

On the 6th October 2013, Sentinelrv created a thread on the official Peercoin forum for the community to discuss the redesign of the official website. He posted:

"Guys, ppcoin.org, as it currently stands, is a problem. I have seen people in chat say that they wouldn't invest in ppc because the website gives off an unprofessional appearance and that it reflects that on the coin. I don't know how many people are affected by this, but it doesn't need to be this way.

I originally posted this thread to gain support for a temp design until we had the time to build a new one, but it seems from the way this thread has gone that people are more interested in fully designing the website, so I've converted this into a planning thread for the redesign.

Go ahead and post any design or feature ideas you can think of. You can leave feedback for ideas or even offer your talents to help with the redesign. The way I see it, this website will act as an information hub that will contribute to many people's understanding of what makes Peercoin better than Bitcoin. That awareness of the benefits of Peercoin is what we want."

On the 15th October 2013, a website graphics designer called Super3 designed, and then proposed, a different layout of the official Peercoin website (see below). The domain address www.ppcoin.org transitioned to www.peercoin.net at this time.

Besides improving the appeal of the official website, Sentinelrv called for volunteers to expand Peercoin operations. He was seeking an array of skills and experience. Code developers, video producers, blog/wiki writers, graphics designers etc. were being sought after.

On the 19th October 2013, prominent members of the Peercoin community took part in an interview with Sunny King. This interview can be read in the appendix of this book from page 149 to page 156. A second interview occurred five days later.

On the 28th October 2013, an exchange called Vault of Satoshi (previously the Toronto Bitcoin Exchange) hosted at https://www.vaultofsatoshi.com/ initiated PPC trading. It was an exchange based in Canada that went live on the 7th October 2013. It closed its doors on the 5th February 2015 due to, as Vault of Satoshi put it, unsustainably insane growth.

Sunny King praised all those who had participated in making Peercoin more professionally appealing to a wider audience. On the technical side, he reported that Peercoin version 0.4 code development was in slow progress. Features from Bitcoin v0.8 were being investigated for potential inclusion.

Major cryptocurrency exchanges offering PPC trading, in late October 2013, were BTC-e, Cryptsy, mcxNOW, Vircurex and Vault of Satoshi.

Other events which occurred during this period included:

- On the 9th September 2013, the exchange Crypto Trade initiated the PPC/USD trading pair.

- On the 30th September 2013, the exchange Cryptsy opened the XPM trading markets section. Alongside others, the XPM/LTC trading pair went live.

- On the 5th October 2013, the US Dollar fiat price of 1 PPC surpassed US$0.50 for the first time.

- On the 18th October 2013, a new official Peercoin Facebook page at www.facebook.com/Peercoin was created.

- On the 22nd October 2013, the official Peercoin YouTube channel at www.youtube.com/OfficialPeercoin was created.

- On the 4th November 2013, a new official (and current) Peercoin Twitter account at www.twitter.com/PeercoinPPC was created. It was initially managed by Peercointalk forum user "MeBeingAwesome".

I.   PEERCOIN TEXT FONT, COLOUR AND THEME CREATED

II.   PPC ATTAINED PARITY WITH THE USD ON 18TH NOVEMBER 2013

III.   ALL TIME 2013/2014 HIGH MARKET CAPITALISATIONS ATTAINED

IV.   BITTREX INITIATED PPC TRADING ON 13TH FEBRUARY 2014

V.   PEER4COMMIT WENT LIVE ON 16TH FEBRUARY 2014

5

2013 PEERCOIN

MARKET CAP RALLY

"2013 has been a fruitful year for cryptocurrencies. Bitcoin woke up from a relatively uneventful 2012 and its marketcap reaches US$10B for the first time. Peercoin achieves 1% of bitcoin marketcap for the first time." - Sunny King

To capitalise on the cryptocurrency market rallies, which began to gain momentum in early November 2013, Sentinelrv made an urgent announcement. On the 7th November 2013, a huge PR (public relations) campaign began. According to Wikipedia, one definition of public relations is:

"The practice of managing the spread of information between an individual or an organisation (such as a business, government agency, or a non-profit organisation) and the public. Public relations may include an organisation or individual gaining exposure to their audiences using topics of public interest and news items that do not require direct payment. This differentiates it from advertising as a form of marketing communications."

All members of the Peercoin community were invited to help out. In particular, JustaBitofTime created many Peercointalk forum threads to motivate and organise community participation in the campaign. It was time to spread awareness about the benefits, vision and innovative characteristics of the Peercoin blockchain.

To complement the Peercoin logo designed by Lightning in July 2013, work began to design a Peercoin text theme. Lightning once again offered his skills to produce variations of the Peercoin text. Different colours and fonts were suggested. On the 10th November 2013, the text font was finalised:

Over the course of the following week, further community input and feedback resulted in the final shade and brightness of the text theme. A leaf had also been designed for the 'I' (see below). The final design is shown on page 60.

During the cryptocurrency market capitalisation rallies in late November 2013, mass media across the globe was beginning to take note. Below are some mass media outlets that reported on Peercoin:

NOVEMBER 20TH 2013: WALL STREET JOURNAL
"Fastcoin? Peercoin? Bitcoin Opens Door to New Currencies"

NOVEMBER 24TH 2013: THE NEW YORK TIMES
"In Bitcoin's Orbit: Rival Virtual Currencies Vie for Acceptance"

NOVEMBER 28TH 2013: THE GUARDIAN UK
"Nine Bitcoin Alternatives for future currency investments"

On the 30th November 2013, the all time 2013 high PPC market capitalisation was attained. It reached a peak at approximately US$187,363,133 at which the US Dollar price per PPC was recorded at US$8.99. Peercoin's market capitalisation surpassed US$100,000,000 the day before.

What follows is a table of historical figures derived from www.coinmarketcap.com showing the astronomical ascent in the US Dollar price per PPC:

	Low US$	Open US$	Close US$	High US$	Market Cap US$
1st Nov 2013	0.371270	0.375176	0.389680	0.394702	8,052,236
18th Nov 2013	0.773334	0.775896	1.13	1.13	23,511,707
28th Nov 2013	3.11	3.57	3.81	4.11	79,261,050
29th Nov 2013	3.65	3.89	7.38	8.19	153,754,699
30th Nov 2013	7.19	7.68	7.75	8.99	161,511,802

As shown in the table above, the US Dollar price per PPC surpassed US$1 for the first time on the 18th November 2013.

On the 4th December 2013, Peercoin community supporter Superppc created and uploaded the first Peercoin promotional video titled "Peercoin vs Bitcoin" to YouTube. Its running time is one minute and twenty four seconds. A screenshot of the last part of the video is shown below.

Other events which occurred during the month of December 2013 included:

- Jordan Lee had made progress with his proposed project Peershares.

- Sunny King and JustaBitofTime were interviewed by CNBC Asia.

- Peercoin was mentioned in the Washington Post Newspaper.

On the 31st December 2013, Sunny King posted his own review of the year 2013:

"2013 has been a fruitful year for cryptocurrencies. Bitcoin woke up from a relatively uneventful 2012 and its marketcap reaches US$10B for the first time. China becomes one of the major markets for cryptocurrencies. Peercoin achieves 1% of bitcoin marketcap for the first time. Numerous currency networks were started, including primecoin from our team, bringing new innovations in proof-of-work consensus algorithms. Meanwhile, ripple introduces the first built-in exchange in a currency network, and establishes itself as the second most valued currency network after bitcoin.

As the competition heats up, 2014 would be an interesting year to look forward to.

Happy New Year!"

On the 9th February 2014, a decision was made to design a visual representation of the Peershares project. Lightning, and others from the community, then helped to design silver versions (see below) of the Peercoin logo. Sentinelrv thanked everyone who had participated and said the following:

"Peershares is supported by Peercoin and proof-of-stake, which makes it an energy efficient program. Because of this, we decided that it should also be represented by the peer to peer symbol we use for Peercoin, similar to how all Apple products (iPod, iPhone, iPad, Mac, etc...) are represented by the Apple logo. The peer to peer symbol ends up representing all energy efficient programs/systems. This shows everyone that both Peercoin and Peershares are from the same people. The double PP symbol fits here because it's submitting "Peer to Peer Coin" with "Peer to Peer Shares". To help differentiate them somewhat though, Peercoin will use the gold symbol while Peershares uses the silver symbol. Both text logos also contain the leaf graphic, Peercoin in the I and Peershares in the a."

On the 13th February 2014, the Bittrex cryptocurrency exchange initiated PPC trading. A single PPC/BTC trading pair went live. This was the opening launch date of the exchange when Bitcoin, Litecoin, Dogecoin, Feathercoin and Vertcoin trading also went live. Bittrex remains operational.

Similar to a previously launched website called tip4commit, Sigmike unveiled Peer4commit on the 16th February 2014. He was motivated to create it after receiving interest from the community and support via donations.

Peer4commit allowed anyone to create, contribute or donate towards Peercoin related projects. Ultimately, it was an organised and user friendly platform to support developers, designers, writers and other people within the Peercoin community achieve their innovative and visionary goals.

On the 18th February 2014, Peerchemist posted his first comment on the official Peercoin forum. He posted the following:

> "Hello, I would like to help. What can I do?
>
> Setting up a Peercoin wallet on Linux Securing your wallet & Backing up your wallet. I also plan to write an extensive guide for minting on RaspberryPi.
>
> Please give me some directions, right now wiki is down so ... what to do?"

On the 25th February 2014, Sunny King announced a tentative PPC version 0.4 release plan. Some members of the community had been concerned about how long it was taking, so he reassured them by saying the release was not far away. Once released, there would be a four week time period to give wallet users, exchanges and other services ample time to upgrade before the protocol switch.

On the 12th March 2014, community member Ötzi posted his first comment on the official Peercoin forum:

"Only Proof-of-Work Mining causes real inflation in Peercoin, minting doesn't, as long as you participate in minting.

Minting ROI is 1% for all holders, so the new coins get distributed proportionally. Imagine the United Kingdom would join the Eurozone. 1 British Pound is worth a little bit more than I Euro. So every holder of British Pounds would have a little "more" money once they have Euros instead of British Pounds. Would that be inflation?

In Peercoin, you only suffer inflation from minting if you do not participate.

So the whole calculation that you want to do is pointless I would say. The interesting part of your question is how many % of Peercoin holders are minting, because that is important for the network stability. Ans that has already been answered."

Other events which occurred during this period included:

- On the 29th November 2013, the BTC-e exchange initiated the PPC/USD trading pair. On this day, the US Dollar price per PPC went over US$5.

- At the end of 2013, the official Peercoin website at www.peercoin.net looked similar to the graphic at the bottom of page 64.

- On the 2nd January 2014, block number 89,059 marked the time at which the number of PPC, generated to date, surpassed 21,000,000.

- On the 3rd January 2014, the all time 2014 high PPC market capitalisation at US$160,881,054 was recorded.

- On the 24th January 2014, Jordan Lee announced that the Peershares project had received approximately US$500,000 in funding.

- On the 29th January 2014, an exchange service called Bittylicious went live for UK customers to easily buy/sell PPC. Bittylicious also added Worldcoin on this day.

I.   PEERCOIN VERSION 0.4.0 RELEASED ON 5TH APRIL 2014

II.   POLONIEX INITIATED PPC TRADING ON 8TH APRIL 2014

III.   FIRST PEERUNITY WALLET CLIENT RELEASED ON 30TH MAY 2014

IV.   PEERCHEMIST ANNOUNCED PEERBOX ON 7TH JUNE 2014

V.   CHRONOS CRYPTO BEGAN TO PRODUCE PEERCOIN RELATED VIDEOS

6

PEERUNITY WALLET
CLIENT RELEASED

*"Peerunity is a Peercoin network-compatible, community-developed wallet
client. The project has been designed to provide people with a stable, secure, and
feature-rich alternative to the Peercoin v0.4.0 reference wallet."*

Following months of code development and testing, Sunny King announced the
release of the first PPC version 0.4 release candidate on the 12th March 2014. He
made it clear that this upgrade was only for deployment on the Peercoin testnet
blockchain. Wallet client users and other service providers had to wait until the 5th
April 2014 for the full release after smooth and successful testing rounds. Peercoin
version 0.4 included:

Improved debug window support
Upgraded stake modifier for possible future p2pool support
getpeerinfo and experimental getblocktemplate support

On the 24th March 2014, the testnet protocol successfully switched to version 0.4
without any major problems. Members of the community were eagerly waiting for
the full official release.

As expected, after the code on testnet had been properly functioning, the official release of Peercoin version 0.4 occurred on the 5th April 2014. It was a mandatory upgrade that had to be installed before the 4th May 2014, otherwise users, exchanges, mining pools and other service providers would have the potential of running a forked version 0.3 Peercoin blockchain.

On the 8th April 2014, the exchange Poloniex initiated PPC trading. The trading pair PPC/BTC went live at https://poloniex.com/exchange/#btc_ppc with immediate effect. Users of this exchange can still trade PPC.

The Poloniex cryptocurrency exchange went live on the 19th January 2014. It is based in the USA. Peercointalk user ppcman said the following:

> "For the longest time, Poloniex.com never traded PPC or Peercoin. I always wanted to ask the site owner why, but I figured eventually the market would dictate that would be a good idea, and it would happen naturally. Well guess what happened this month?
>
> Poloniex.com now carries PPC / Peercoin as a trading pair on their exchange."

On the 12th April 2014, Peershares architect Jordan Lee notified the Peercoin community of a future release of a community driven wallet client called Peerunity (to exist alongside the core qt wallet client). It would support both Peercoin and Peershares. Everyone was invited to contribute to its development. Jordan Lee had earlier advertised for two skilled C++ developers to join the Peershares development team.

For the remainder of April 2014, and into May 2014, Peerunity underwent regular testing phases. Technically minded members from the Peercoin community were especially encouraged to contribute. A new thread at www.peercointalk.org was created for dedicated Peerunity discussion.

Besides code development, the Peercoin community had been busy designing a visual representation for the Peerunity wallet client. Peercointalk user mhps suggested the idea to combine the gold from Peercoin and the silver from Peershares. He considered this as symbolising the merging of the two. After several weeks, the final Peerunity designs were chosen:

On the 30th May 2014, the first release (version 0.1.0) of the Peerunity wallet client was made available by the Peerunity development team via official download links and on the Peerunity Github repository website for Windows, Linux and Mac. The initial description of the release was:

"Peerunity is a Peercoin network-compatible, community-developed wallet client.

The project has been designed to provide people with a stable, secure, and feature-rich alternative to the Peercoin v0.4.0 reference wallet (http://github.com/ppcoin/ppcoin)."

On the 5th June 2014, Jordan Lee announced the name of the Peershares implementation that his team had been working on. The NuBits project was initially described, by him, as an upcoming ground breaking release. He expected its release very soon (see NuBits logo above).

On the 7th June 2014, Peerchemist announced the Peerbox project. He had been investigating ways to address the security and privacy concerns regarding cryptocurrencies, especially those based on proof of stake timestamping. He said:

> "Peercoin utilises a process called minting that requires that a wallet is unlocked and then connected to at least 8 peers on the network, each and everyone of those peers now knows the IP of person minting, thus enabling attack vector.
>
> Running a full node is even more risky, now you connect to 20-70 peers with port 9901 forwarded. That means this port, on which Peercoin wallet is running is now completely open to anyone on the Internet, exposing it to attackers. Knowing this people tend to avoid minting and risk entire network security by doing so."

Ultimately, the goal of the project had been set to provide a maximum security platform for minting PPC and for running nodes. Peerchemist also stated a secondary goal; to provide a plug & play platform for running PPC nodes.

On the 17th June 2014, based on consensus of project leaders in the community, Sunny King announced that Sigmike had become a PPC core developer. He would henceforth share responsibility with Sunny King for maintaining and developing the Peercoin network protocol. Sigmike had been a key member of the Peershares and Peerunity projects. Sunny King was also quoted as saying:

> "There are many more talented developers/contributors in the community project teams, so we are continuing to evaluate and seek recommendations. Some of the key members are focusing on the respective project currently but could be joining the core-dev team at a later date. It's very nice to see the growth of peercoin dev community and the quality work being produced."

As an important part of increasing Peercoin awareness and adoption, Peercointalk user river announced the launch of the Peercoin Marketing Fund on the 30th June 2014. It would allow marketing to be done by the community, for the community. Members of the community became able to freely submit proposals, and then potentially receive funding (funds stored on Peer4commit). River and Cybnate were initially responsible for safeguarding funds.

On the 13th July 2014, as part of the 'Peercoin Community Video Project', Chronos Crypto uploaded a 38 minute video titled "Intro to Peercoin" to YouTube. Sentinelrv described it as impressive and informative.

Six days later, a brand new Peercoin promotional video was uploaded to the official Peercoin YouTube channel. It became the new video to describe the Peercoin blockchain. A screenshot from the video is:

Other interesting and intriguing projects were being submitted to the Peer4commit website. Since being established in February 2014, it had become an important hub for proposing, organising and contributing to Peercoin related community projects.

Other events which occurred during this period included:

- On the 22nd April 2014, The Rock Trading exchange initiated PPC trading by opening the https://www.therocktrading.com/en/offers/PPCEUR market.

- On the 13th May 2014, the Coinnext exchange initiated PPC trading.

- On the 18th June 2014, the Peershares development team proudly announced the release of version 0.1.0 of the Peershares template demonstration network for Windows, Linux and Mac.

- On the 18th June 2014, an exchange called CCEDK initiated PPC trading.

- On the 23rd June 2014, a Peercoin block explorer went live at the domain address https://peerchain.co thanks to Peercointalk user JetJet13.

- On the 7th July 2014, the Primecoin blockchain turned one year old.

I.   FIRST PPC ANDROID WALLET RELEASED ON 11TH SEPTEMBER 2014

II.   NUBITS BLOCKCHAIN LAUNCHED ON 23RD SEPTEMBER 2014

III.   PEERUNITY VERSION 0.1.1 RELEASED ON 11TH OCTOBER 2014

IV.   CHRONOS CRYPTO PRODUCED MORE PEERCOIN VIDEOS

V.   CRYPTO MARKET CAPITALISATIONS SHARPLY DECLINED IN 2014

7

FURTHER PEERCOIN DEVELOPMENT

"On the 23rd September 2014, the NuBits blockchain launched. It was the first major DAC project in the Peercoin ecosystem"

During the spring of 2014, various Peercoin related projects were being worked on by skilled members of the community. Sunny King was very pleased to see how the project had grown since its inception. Funds were being raised via the website www.peer4commit.com to help developers, content creators and contributors achieve their goals. Sunny King was quoted as saying:

"Our development community has grown quite a bit compared to last year, thanks to the tireless and selfless teamwork of many of you. I am amazed at what our community has achieved, and honoured to express my appreciation of all your great works."

Sunny King had recently been interviewed by Sean Mikha from the online 'Let's Talk Bitcoin Network' website. An article was subsequently published titled "The Real Sunny" on the 21st July 2014.

On the 9th August 2014, for the first time since the 21st November 2013, the price of each PPC went below US$1. Sunny King, given recent market losses since the beginning of the year, reminded investors in PPC and XPM to be aware of high price volatility (invest only what you can afford to lose).

Ten days later, members of the community acknowledged the second anniversary of the Peercoin blockchain. Block number 128,270 marked the time at which the blockchain had been operational for at least two years (see below).

Block #128,270 (Reward 0.07 PPC) August 19th 2014 at 18:23:04 UTC

On the 26th August 2014, the Peerbox logo (see below) was published. People were encouraged to follow Peerchemist for updates on Peerbox development (the plug and play self-contained OS dedicated to PPC minting on RaspberryPi).

On the 11th September 2014, MatthewLM notified the Peercoin community that he had released the first ever Peercoin Android wallet. He uploaded the application immediately to the Google Play Store. Potential users were advised to use it at their own risk. The source code had not yet been checked (beta software).

Nearly one year since Jordan Lee published the preliminary design for Peershares, and after funding was finalised in January 2014 to accelerate its development, the NuBits release date was announced on the 15th September 2014. NuBits had been scheduled to launch at approximately 14:00 UTC on the 23rd September 2014.

Jordan Lee also said the following:

"Our solution completely solves the volatility problem cryptocurrencies have experienced. It does so with zero counterparty risk using a decentralized network. Much of the network revenue will be delivered to shareholders in the form of Peercoins. The network is an exciting advance I am pleased to have the opportunity to unveil."

As scheduled, the NuBits blockchain launched on the 23rd September 2014. The first two cryptocurrency exchanges to initiate USNBT trading were CCEDK and Bter (both promised to add NuBits before its launch). Sunny King congratulated the NuBits team for creating the first major DAC project in the Peercoin ecosystem.

On the 11th October 2014, Peerunity version 0.1.1 was released. It featured more user interface (UI) enhancements and code fixes. It was not a mandatory upgrade, but introduced new features to extend the functionality of the client.

Peerunity version 0.1.1 included the following features:

- The ability to display the probability of minting Peercoins within a time frame for different input transactions via the 'minting' tab.

- Multi-signature address support.

- The ability to clear orphan minted/mined blocks.

Since July 2014, Chronos Crypto had been producing and uploading Peercoin related videos to YouTube. These videos are highly praised as being very informative and which help newbies in the community understand the concepts of mining, minting and using the wallet client software. By the 26th November 2014, Chronos Crypto had uploaded eleven videos:

10th July 2014	Review: Sprite's Peercoin Medallion
13th July 2014	Intro to Peercoin
29th July 2014	Earn 10 Peercoin with your Raspberry Pi
29th July 2014	Ripple Giveaway for Developers
6th September 2014	Peercoin Mining Overview
6th September 2014	Getting Started with Peerunity
6th September 2014	Peercoin Minting Overview
6th September 2014	Peercoin Minting Tutorial
16th November 2014	Paper Wallets Walkthrough
16th November 2014	Paper Wallets Overview
26th November 2014	Review: Wooden Wallets

On the 6th December 2014, the Cryptopia exchange initiated PPC trading. Several trading pairs, including PPC/BTC, PPC/LTC and PPC/DOGE, went live.

During 2014, all cryptocurrencies, which existed at the time of the 2013 market rally, had plunged in value. Peercoin had descended from the top four to tenth position (see table below) in terms of market capitalisation. Other blockchains, being described as 2.0 projects, had overtaken Peercoin. They included BitShares, Nxt, Stellar and Dogecoin.

Rank	Date	Market Cap US$	Price US$	Volume US$
4	5th January 2014	152,073,508	7.23	5,371,518
10	28th December 2014	12,955,668	0.589649	70,412

Towards the end of the year, Sunny King informed the community that Sigmike had been making significant progress on a feature called cold-minting. Sigmike had completed its backend code. Sunny King described the feature as follows:

> "It allows for minting with special mint-only key, while the corresponding spending key can be stored in a cold wallet. This safeguards the coins of a minting wallet from hackers who gain unauthorized access to user's system. The feature will be under review and testing in the following weeks."

Other events which occurred during this period included:

- On the 9th September 2014, Peerbox version 0.22 was released.

- On the 23rd September 2014, a new official Peercoin Bitcointalk thread was created at 02:17:10 UTC by Sentinelrv. Despite its creation, most community discussion still continued to take place at www.peercointalk.org.

- On the 23rd September 2014, Cryptsy initiated the PPC/USD trading pair.

- On the 14th October 2014, Peerbox version 0.23 was released.

- On the 26th October 2014, the Peercoin network protocol surpassed 400 full single nodes.

- On the 17th November 2014, The Rock Trading exchange initiated the https://www.therocktrading.com/en/offers/PPCBTC market.

- On the 18th November 2014, Peerbox version 0.24 was released. It made it possible for users to activate 2FA for extra security.

I. NEW PEERUNITY THEME PROPOSED ON 19TH JANUARY 2015

II. PEERCOIN FIRST YEAR HISTORY BOOK PUBLISHED ON AMAZON

III. BTC38 AND BTC-e HIGHEST PPC VOLUME EXCHANGES IN JUNE 2015

IV. PEERCOIN BLOCKCHAIN SIZE COMPARISON

V. FUZZYBEAR RECEIVED THE PEERCOIN MARKETING FUND

8

A QUIET PHASE
FOR PEERCOIN

"Peercoin is a backbone currency used to settle and secure larger sums of money, not used for day to day small transactions at high volume." - Sunny King

Since the Peercoin blockchain launched in August 2012, the annualised inflation rate of the number of PPC generated had been decreasing. Firstly, this was due to the decreasing proportion of proof of work blocks. Secondly, the mining reward of proof of work blocks had been decreasing due to increased hashrate processing power committed by miners.

On the 1st January 2015, the annualised inflation rate for Peercoin was recorded at below 5% (see table below). For comparison, corresponding figures for Bitcoin and Litecoin, at this time, were approximately 10% and 44% respectively.

Dates	Annualised Inflation
1st January 2013—1st January 2014	+39.1%
19th August 2013—19th August 2014	+8.12%
1st January 2014—1st January 2015	+4.71%

Block #153,009 (Reward 82.58 PPC) January 11th 2015 at 00:35:18 UTC

On the 11th January 2015, the total number of PPC, generated to date, surpassed 22,000,000 at block number 153,009 (see above).

To make the Peerunity community wallet client more appealing and user friendly, SigmundAlpha proposed a new theme design on the 19th January 2015. Sentinelrv praised the new design as a great visual improvement over the original theme. It would not be implemented into the client until the release of Peerunity version 0.2.0 on the 26th March 2016.

A screenshot of the new Peerunity wallet client theme design is shown below.

On the 25th February 2015, an active core member of the Peercoin community called Nagalim introduced himself on the Peercointalk forum:

> "I've kind of fallen in love with peercoin and nu over the last year. I could hype till the cows come home, but it's the connection to the people that really drives my interest I think. That we can measure the security of our network based off how distributed the wealth is just makes my mind reel with implications. If every person on earth had just ~0.003 PPC, we'd be fully distributed. Anyway, glad to be a part of the community."

On the 30th April 2015, the US Dollar price per PPC attained its all time 2015 low. Also shown in the table below, the all time 2015 high was recorded on the 10th July 2015 at US$1.02 per PPC.

Date	PPC (US$)	PPC (BTC Sat)	Volume (US$)	Market Cap (US$)
30th April 2015	0.211304	93,820	9,796	4,707,000
10th July 2015	1.02	372,900	2,993,140	22,839,000

Some members of the community were concerned about the high proportion of PPC trading occurring on the BTC-e exchange (see page 84). They wanted to see diversification of trading to other exchanges such as Bittrex and Poloniex.

On the 20th May 2015, after several months of research and content writing, a book based on the first year history of Peercoin was published on Amazon:

What follows is a snapshot of the top five cryptocurrency exchanges, in terms of PPC trading volume, on the 14th June 2015:

Exchange	Trading Pair	Volume (US$)	PPC (US$)	% Volume
BTC38	PPC/CNY	34,707	0.319892	29.44
BTC-e	PPC/BTC	34,036	0.317590	28.87
BTC-e	PPC/USD	20,384	0.322000	17.29
CCEDK	PPC/USD	14,423	0.321999	12.23
Jubi	PPC/CNY	11,234	0.323124	9.53
Cryptsy	PPC/BTC	2,449	0.322197	2.08

On the 10th July 2015, according to the https://bitinfocharts.com ranking website, the blockchain sizes of Bitcoin, Dogecoin, Litecoin and Peercoin were compared (see below). It was clear that the size of the Peercoin blockchain was less than 1% the size of the Bitcoin blockchain. A major contributing factor to this small figure is the 0.01 PPC transaction fee that minimises the number of transactions sent. Sunny King reaffirmed Peercoin's goal as a backbone currency used to settle and secure larger sums of money, as opposed to day to day small transactions at high volume.

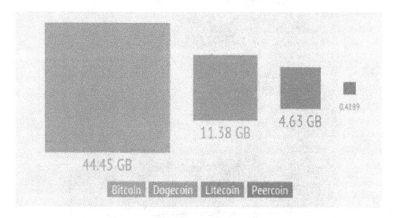

Over one year after the Peercoin Marketing Fund went live, both Cybnate and River decided to relinquish their responsible of running it. They asked prominent members of the community to run it instead, and FuzzyBear said that he would.

However, the rules stated that two people had to run it. On the 6th September 2015, in order to move forward, a vote began to decide what to do with the PPC held in the Peercoin Marketing Fund.

On the 7th October 2015, FuzzyBear was unanimously chosen to receive the marketing fund. He replied by posting:

> "Hey all, Many thanks again for your votes of confidence :) really gives me a boost to get such feedback. Sorry had some Internet issues but looks like I am back up and running now. I have set up a peer4commit fund to hold the marketing funds in and a donation address PGDC2CH3DroK66H6sP4WMh7aK521PMwBFN is ready to go.
> https://peer4commit.com/projects/161
>
> Initial thoughts are to create a brand of Peercoin clothing that I will be selling though the forum / subdomain and use us as Peercoin adverts. Any sale of clothes will be of course in Peercoins and hence used to boost the pot back up. I am keen to see blog writers and radio presenters do talks about Peercoin so I am open to suggestions from writers. I would also like to see this fund used to promote the Peerbox project more in the Rasp Pi scene. The fund IMO should also be used to send representatives from the community to Bitcoin / altcoin conferences etc but there needs to be an agenda for the individual going and ideally a talk / presentation given."

Following on from months of code development, and weeks of testing and review, Sunny King announced that the first Peercoin version 0.5 release candidate had been uploaded for download (testnet deployment) on the 7th November 2015.

Other events which occurred during this period included:

- On the 5th January 2015, the Yobit exchange initiated PPC trading.

- On the 26th March 2015, Peercoin Android wallet v2.3 was released.

- On the 6th September 2015, Peercoin Android wallet v3.0 was released.

- On the 6th September 2015, the https://chainz.cryptoid.info/ppc block explorer went live.

- On the 23rd September 2015, the USNBT unit of account for NuBits had sustained parity with the US Dollar for one year.

I.   **PEERCOIN BLOCKCHAIN FORKED ON 9TH NOVEMBER 2015**

II.   **PEERCOIN VERSION 0.4.2 RELEASED ON 8TH DECEMBER 2015**

III.   **PEERCOIN VERSION 0.5.2 RELEASED ON 5TH MARCH 2016**

IV.   **PEERCOIN BLOCKCHAIN SWITCHED TO V0.5 ON 26TH APRIL 2016**

V.   **LAST PEERUNITY CLIENT VERSION RELEASED ON 6TH MAY 2016**

9

ACCIDENTAL FORKS AND

THE SWITCH TO V0.5

"On the 26th April 2016, the Peercoin blockchain switched to v0.5 protocol."

Unexpectedly, the Peercoin blockchain suffered a fork issue on the 9th November 2015. Sunny King described what had happened in his weekly update to the community:

> **"Many peercoin users have experienced 'invalid checkpoint error' in the last couple of days, this is due to an attack on the network based on an exploit of an openssl library cross-platform issue. It caused peercoin blockchain to fork into two chains:**
>
> **one on v0.4.0 linux 64 bit**
>
> **one on v0.4.0 linux 32 bit and windows."**

On the 10th November 2015, a Peercoin (version 0.4.1) release candidate was made available for impacted wallet client users. Sunny King reiterated the fact that Linux 32 bit and Windows wallet client users did not need to upgrade. He also advised users to avoid transacting PPC before the upgrade had been performed.

High praise was given to community members who swiftly responded to the fork issue. In particular, Sigmike was applauded for his dedication to solve the issue and provide the necessary hot fix release (on the 10th November 2015).

After several weeks of code testing, Peercoin version 0.4.2 was released on the 8th December 2015. It was described as a maintenance release. Wallet client users impacted by the blockchain fork event were advised to upgrade. Version 0.4.2 had become the current release.

On the 3rd January 2016, Peercoin was ranked on www.coinmarketcap.com as one of the top ten cryptocurrencies in terms of market capitalisation. What follows is a table showing the top ten on this day:

Rank		Ticker	Market Cap US$	Price US$
1	Bitcoin	BTC	6,467,437,080	430.01
2	Ripple	XRP	201,799,631	0.006017
3	Litecoin	LTC	152,873,521	3.48
4	Ethereum	ETH	73,843,278	0.971905
5	Dash	DASH	19,794,713	3.24
6	Dogecoin	DOGE	14,940,681	0.000146
7	Peercoin	PPC	9,756,959	0.426281
8	BitShares	BTS	8,591,688	0.003386
9	Stellar	XLM	8,436,465	0.001744
10	Nxt	NXT	6,863,998	0.006864

Major exchanges on which Peercoin was trading included BTC-e, Cryptsy, Poloniex and Bittrex.

On the 15th January 2016, the Cryptsy cryptocurrency exchange ceased all trading operations. Its users had been able to trade PPC since the 23rd May 2013. Unfortunately, many users of Cryptsy found it impossible to withdraw their cryptocurrencies before the shutdown.

On the 23rd January 2016, Hrobeers posted his first comment on the official Peercoin forum:

> "Hi all, Like you, I love the blockchain! I own some BTC from right before the 2013 peak, so that's great. After figuring out the Proof Of Work principle, I figured out that PoS is way more interesting, so I found this wonderful coin and it's wonderful community. I hope to interact with you guys so..."

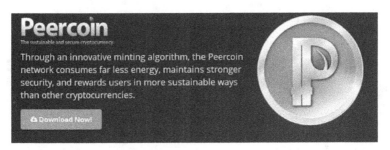

On the 5th March 2016, Peercoin version 0.5.2 was released. Wallet client users had to upgrade before a stated tentative deadline on the 25th April 2016. Support for Peercoin version 0.4.2 had ended. Sunny King emphasised the importance of notifying as many service providers (exchanges, mining pools, etc.) that a mandatory upgrade had been released.

Five days later, the all time 2016 high PPC market capitalisation was attained at approximately US$12,940,000 according to the www.coinmarketcap.com ranking website. Figures derived from this website are:

	Low US$	Open US$	Close US$	High US$	Volume US$
10th March 2016	0.494883	0.543622	0.520476	0.562379	330,442

On the 21st March 2016, Peercoin version 0.5.3 was released. It introduced a fix to a 'transaction display' code bug found in the previous version. The deadline to upgrade by the 25th April 2016 still applied.

Also, an upgrade (version 0.2.0) for the Peerunity wallet client was released on the 26th March 2016. Peerunity had become compatible with the version 0.5.3 Peercoin network protocol.

Sentinelrv pointed out that the recently released Peerunity upgrade had integrated a new visual theme (see below) with the Peercoin branded colours. He also said:

> "For those unfamiliar with Peerunity, it is an easier to use community client which offers extra features that the core client doesn't, such as enabling minting from the menu and other features. You can download at the link below, as well as see screenshots of the updated theme. Once again, the OS X version is still being worked on."

https://github.com/Peerunity/Peerunity/releases/

On the 1st April 2016, Peerbox version 0.5 was released by Peerchemist. He had revamped its functionality and promised to keep improving it. He posted the following announcement:

> "For those unfamiliar, the ultimate goal of Peerbox is to provide a maximum security platform for safely minting and running Peercoin nodes. With this release, Peerbox is no longer an independent operating system and is now designed as an add on for Debian.
>
> This new architecture enables stability, ease of installation and use and ease of maintenance. What is most important, the new Peerbox enables even less technology savvy people to use it, as it features a graphical user interface for the first time. Tor support for full nodes is also included. Users can now transform their Raspberry Pi into a Peerbox in minutes and not lose any of the functionality they are used to."

On the 26th April 2016, the Peercoin blockchain successfully switched to version 0.5 protocol. Both Sentinelrv and Peerchemist had been actively notifying service providers before the switch occurred.

On the following day, Sunny King informed the community that the Peerunity wallet client had forked (block number 233,762) from the main Peercoin blockchain. A hot fix was quickly released (version 0.2.1) thanks to the Peerunity team.

Once again, the Peercoin blockchain accidently forked on the 5th May 2016. Both Windows and 32 bit Linux wallet clients were impacted (related to the fork in November 2015) at block number 234,613. Wallet client users were unable to download the full blockchain (synchronise) to their computers.

On the 6th May 2016, thanks to Sigmike and other competent community members, Peercoin version 0.5.4 and Peerunity 0.2.2 (last ever Peerunity upgrade) were released. Both upgrades resolved the earlier synchronisation issues.

In addition to the above releases, Peerchemist published a whitepaper on Github detailing a new project called PeerAssets on the 6th May 2016. PeerAssets would enable the issuing of, then allow subsequent transactions of, assets on top the Peercoin blockchain.

Other events which occurred during this period included:

- On the 14th January 2016, Sigmike announced that he had coded a faucet at http://peercoinfaucet.com (it had been active for about one week).

- On the 16th January 2016, an online cryptocurrency news website called Coin Telegraph published an article titled "Peercoin—Rise and Fall. Is It Rising Again?"

- On the 20th February 2016, the number of PPC generated to date surpassed 23,000,000 at block number 222,475 via PoW (Ecoining).

- On the 6th April 2016, an exchange based in The Netherlands called LiteBit initiated PPC trading. A single trading market located at the domain address https://www.litebit.eu/en/buy/peercoin went live.

I.   TEAM OF DEVELOPERS WORKING HARD ON PEERCOIN PROJECTS

II.   PEERCOIN TEAM INTERVIEWED BY COINDESK ON 14TH JULY 2016

III.   PEERCOIN CHAT SERVICE LAUNCHED ON 6TH AUGUST 2016

IV.   PEERCOIN 4TH ANNIVERSARY CELEBRATED ON 19TH AUGUST 2016

V.   PEERCOIN LOGO REBRANDED AND MODERNISED

10

THE REBIRTH
OF PEERCOIN

"Peercoin's underlying purpose is to provide the ability to store value in an inexpensive to maintain crypto network which prioritises security, decentralisation and scarcity over speed, low fees and high transaction volumes." - Sentinelrv

Around the time the Peercoin blockchain switched to version 0.5 protocol, a team of developers (Peerchemist, Hrobeers and Saeveritt) were beginning to form within the Peercoin ecosystem. Projects dedicated to improving and taking Peercoin to the next level included the following:

- **Peerbox:** a secure and private way to mint PPC units of account by using a plug and play self-contained OS dedicated to Peercoin minting on Raspberry Pi.

- **PeerAssets:** a blockchain protocol which enables its users to issue or transact assets such as bonds, equities or shares etc.

- **PeerKeeper:** an advanced thin based browser web wallet.

- **Peercoin Wisdom:** a website focused on increasing Peercoin exposure.

It was the case that some of the projects had already been released, while others were still under active development. Peercoin had entered the early stages of a rebirth or transitional phase.

Sentinelrv understood, as did many others in the Peercoin community, that funding had been lacking for a year or so. He politely asked the community, especially large PPC holders or investors, to support the innovation around Peercoin:

"Funding the developers that are responsible for the most promising projects
that are supporting Peercoin is the best way to see your investment grow. Without
proper funding, it will be a struggle for our developers to bring Peercoin up to
speed with the rest of the crypto world."

Block # 419,999 (Reward 25 BTC) July 9th 2016 at 17:41:53 UTC

Block #420,000 (Reward 12.5 BTC) July 9th 2016 at 17:46:13 UTC

For the second time in history, the proof of work block reward of the Bitcoin blockchain suddenly halved (see above). Similar to the case in November 2012, Bitcoin miners found themselves receiving half the profits. Some miners then decided to mine Peercoin instead.

On the 14th July 2016, Jacob Donnelly from the online cryptocurrency news website CoinDesk interviewed Sunny King and other members of the team including Sentinelrv, Peerchemist, Hrobeers and Saeveritt. The full transcript of the interview can be read in the appendix of this book from pages 169 to 192. Later on, Sunny King said:

"We did a great interview as a team with CoinDesk this week. I liked it
very much, as in the past most of those are me alone. Thanks team!"

On the 6th August 2016, Peerchemist created a new Peercoin related service at http://chat.peerbox.me by using open source Rocket.chat software. He hoped it would provide a better method for the Peercoin community to talk.

Beginning in June 2016, Peercointalk user ppcman had an idea to mark the fourth anniversary of the Peercoin blockchain. He began to plan and organise several celebratory events, including:

- Securing Peercoin's presence on the popular online Beyond Bitcoin Radio Show by talking privately with Fuzzy (not to be confused with FuzzyBear!).

- Inspiring the community to produce a Peercoin celebratory banner. Special thanks were given to Sentinelrv and Saeveritt for creating it (see below).

On the 13th August 2016, Peercointalk user ppcman also held a "Peercoin Photo/Meme" contest. Members of the community had until the 21st August 2016 to submit photos before a winner was announced.

On the 19th August 2016, the Peercoin team took part in the scheduled Beyond Bitcoin Radio Show. Sentinelrv, Hrobeers, Chronos Crypto, Intelliguy and others talked during the one hour and forty five minute segment. It was hosted by Intelliguy. Different topics were discussed including the advantages of Peercoin over other blockchains, the history of Peercoin and what to expect next. Extensive use of http://chat.peerbox.me was made after the show to discuss further topics.

What follows is the opening Beyond Bitcoin segment audio speech by Sentinelrv:

> "When Sunny King originally developed Peercoin, he had a very specific long-term vision of a network that is designed for maximum decentralisation and security. Peercoin's underlying purpose is to provide the ability to store value in an inexpensive to maintain crypto network which prioritises security, decentralisation and scarcity over speed, low fees and high transaction volumes. This is the definition of a back-bone currency."

As shown below, the Peercoin blockchain turned four years old as soon as block number 253,728 was timestamped:

Block #253,728 (Reward 2.59 PPC) August 19th 2016 2016 at 18:23:11 UTC

During August 2016, discussions had been taking place on the http://chat.peerbox.me general channel about rebranding Peercoin. Sentinelrv, Saeveritt, Hrobeers, Peerchemist and River agreed to drop the two 'P's symbol in favour of shifting solely to the leaf symbol to best represent the coin. Sentinelrv was aware that the two 'P's logo had served Peercoin well, but it was time for a new image to support the rebirth of the project. In particular, Sentinelrv pointed out that the logo currently being used could not be clearly recognised when reduced (16 x 16) in size.

On the 8th September 2016, different shades of the green leaf were proposed for the community to vote on. Three colour sample options were initially posted (sample #4 was later proposed by Irritant) as shown immediately below:

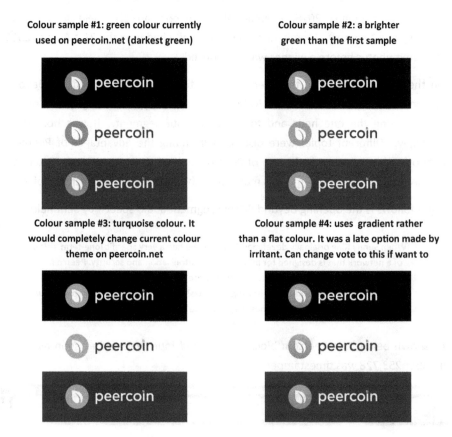

Colour sample #1: green colour currently used on peercoin.net (darkest green)

Colour sample #2: a brighter green than the first sample

Colour sample #3: turquoise colour. It would completely change current colour theme on peercoin.net

Colour sample #4: uses gradient rather than a flat colour. It was a late option made by irritant. Can change vote to this if want to

On the 13th September 2016, Sentinelrv announced that the Peercoin team had acquired the https://peercoin.org domain address. Long time PPC supporter Superppc, who created the first Peercoin promotional video back in December 2013, answered the community's call during the previous month. Superppc had successfully negotiated with the domain address owner, then settled on a mutually satisfactory purchase price. The https://peercoin.org domain address had become free for the community to use. Sentinelrv, Peerchemist, Saeveritt, Nagalim and others praised Superppc for his great generosity.

On the following day, the voting for the new Peercoin logo ended. Two days later, Sentinelrv disclosed the results. Sample #2 won with 14 votes (ten votes more than sample #4 in second place). All members of the Peercoin team voted for sample #2. Sentinelrv said the following:

> "I will now take the next steps, which is to have my designer develop a
> full set for #2, just as he did for the previous logo. This will end up costing me
> a couple hundred dollars, so Peercoin donations are appreciated to help me pay
> for it. My PPC address is in my signature. Thanks to anyone that helps out!"

On the 5th October 2016, several Peercoin social media channels had already been updated to reflect the new Peercoin theme and colours:

Twitter:	https://twitter.com/PeercoinPPC
Facebook:	https://www.facebook.com/Peercoin
Google+:	https://plus.google.com/+PeercoinNet
YouTube:	https://www.youtube.com/user/peercoin
Peercoin.chat:	https://peercoin.chat/channel/general

Over the following weeks, two other Peercoin related online resources were updated too:

- On the 6th October 2016, it was reported that the Peercoin website at https://peercoin.net had been fully revamped (see image below).

- On the 12th October 2016, the official Peercoin Subreddit located at https://www.reddit.com/r/peercoin was updated. Also, it was updated to include more sections and useful links.

On the 28th October 2016, a Telegram group was created at https://telegram.me/peercoinppc for seamless community chat. It was known that other cryptocurrency projects had been utilising Telegram too. Bots were setup to allow messages to be posted simultaneously on https://peercoin.chat and Telegram.

On the 28th November 2016, core member Nagalim published an article on the Peercoin Medium channel titled "Building Spires in Sunny Kingdoms" in which he covered a historical re-cap of Peercoin so far. The introductory segment of the article is as follows:

> "Sunny King (SK) and Scott Nadal pioneered the Proof of Stake (PoS) protocol via Peercoin (PPC) in August 2012, building off the work previously done by Satoshi Nakamoto in creating Bitcoin and Proof of Work (PoW). The initial purpose of PoS was to greatly reduce the energy cost of maintaining a decentralized ledger by replacing the anti-sybil mechanism of energy consumption with that of stake in an established system. The philosophical consequences were deep as Peercoin united the interests of the coin users and the network validators, reducing the governance gap between those that transact in the currency and those that validate transactions (txns). The result has been a steady agreement over the txn fee of 0.01 PPC/kb, burned out of supply, that acts as both a cost to individuals and a reward to the entire network for filling and maintaining blockchain space."

Other events which occurred during this period included:

- On the 10th June 2016, the peg between the US Dollar and the USNBT unit of account collapsed. Interest in NuBits had become negligible before this event. The Peercoin team later described NuBits as a "brain drain" of resources and developer talent from the Peercoin project itself.

- On the 14th June 2016, an exchange called Southxchange initiated PPC trading. Two trading pairs, PPC/BTC and PPC/DASH, went live.

- On the 16th September 2016, Peerchemist announced that the Peercoin chat service at https://chat.peerbox.me had changed its domain name to https://peercoin.chat

- On the 7th December 2016, the number of Peercoin Twitter followers surpassed 5,000 for the first time.

- On the 20th December 2016, the all time 2016 low price per PPC was recorded at US$0.210275 (did not go below this figure in 2017 and 2018).

I. REVAMPED PEERCOIN FORUM LAUNCHED ON 9TH JANUARY 2017

II. FIRST RFC PROTOCOL IMPROVEMENT PROPOSAL SUBMITTED

III. INDICIUM PRE-ANNOUNCED ON 7TH MARCH 2017

IV. PEERCHEMIST BECAME PROJECT LEADER ON 5TH APRIL 2017

V. PEERCOIN CORE TEAM ROLES DEFINED

11

NEW PEERCOIN
TEAM FORMED

"Sunny King approves of Peerchemist in taking this official role and has offered him his full support. Sunny will of course continue his current role within the dev team as founder and lead developer of the Peercoin protocol." - Sentinelrv

After the Christmas and New Year holidays, work resumed to make Peercoin more appealing to people inside and outside the cryptocurrency space. Sunny King was proud to announce that both Peerchemist and Hrobeers had recently joined the core development team. It was recognition for their great contributions so far.

On the 4th January 2017, the developers decided to begin using RFCs (Request for Comments) as a standard for submitting protocol improvement proposals to facilitate open source code development. On this day, the first RFC (RFC-0001) was titled "Exponential PoS Target for Block Time Stabilisation" on the relevant https://github.com/peercoin/rfcs/ Github repository website. It was authored by Hrobeers and summarised as follows:

"Stabilizing the Proof-of-Stake block timing by multiplying the hash target using an exponential function of time since the last PoS block."

New Peercoin Team Formed

On the 9th January 2017, after being in development for almost two years, a brand new Peercoin forum website was launched in beta for all existing members. It was described as lighter, cleaner and more mobile phone friendly than the previous forum (see previous forum interface below). Sentinelrv was quoted as saying:

> "I reached out to Jooize on July 22nd, 2016 and told him of my intention
> to move forward with migrating the Peercointalk forum to discourse and I asked
> him for his help. He was more than happy to help the community with this task
> and for the past 5 months we've worked together to bring it to you. Jooize
> handled the technical side while I handled the organizing."

After testing, the new forum https://talk.peercoin.net went live for new user registrations on the 14th January 2017. Sentinelrv admitted that the migration of all content from https://peercointalk.org to https://talk.peercoin.net had been a massive task. He posted the following as a thank you:

> " I would like to personally thank Fuzzy for putting up with me bugging him
> about this for the last 2 years as well as allowing us the opportunity to improve
> out public image. This would not have been possible if he did not give us a copy of
> the database to do the migration. I'd also like to thank @jooize for all his help,
> @sigmike for the fixes on the script, @peerchemist for setting up the server,
> @MAL and @Super3 for helping out with changing the DNS settings. None of this
> could have been achieved without their help."

On the 10th February 2017, the first Peercoin team update was published on the new forum and other related social media channels. Sunny King had, for a couple of months, stopped posting his weekly updates. It was another sign that the new Peercoin team was taking on more responsibility for the project. Sentinelrv would, from this point on, post updates to keep the community informed on progress.

On the 7th March 2017, Nagalim pre-announced the first PeerAssets DAC (Decentralised Autonomous Company) called Indicium:

"Indicium is an upcoming DAC (decentralized autonomous company) centered around the creation of cryptocurrency ETFs (Exchange Traded Funds). The DAC will issue its tokens via the PeerAssets protocol on the Peercoin blockchain, giving great flexibility to the company as a blockchain agnostic entity and acting as the first application of the new protocol. Indicium seeks to apply proven mathematical re-balancing algorithms used by the financial industry to form a robust basket of cryptocurrencies.

Indicium will greatly mature the crypto-marketplace by providing a hedge with reduced volatility while also outperforming the Bitcoin market in long term trends. This will be accomplished using on-exchange trading bots and holding multi-signature reserves off-exchange with all operations controlled by an elected board of managers.

The founding team is deeply intertwined with the Peercoin and PeerAssets development team, giving proof of technical expertise involved in this project. A small scale initial public offering will serve to acquire development funds and distribute indX tokens used to vote and elect the board of directors. Profit can be reinvested into the company or given as dividends for a return on investment. More information will come out soon."

Besides core developers working on other Peercoin projects, Sunny King announced he had opened up the Peercoin version 0.6 Github repository hub for developers to contribute to by testing the code, submitting improvements and reporting code bugs.

Other events which occurred during March 2017 were:

- On the 17th March 2017, the second round of PeerAssets community testing went live after the successful first round the previous month.

- The recently created Peercoin Medium account was branded as "Peercoin Pulse". It became recognised as the official Peercoin blog.

On the 22nd March 2017, the second and third Request for Comments were created for technically minded community members to consider and contribute to:

RFC-0002—COINSTAKE TRANSACTION SPLIT (authored by Hrobeers)

Splitting the coinstake transaction into a monetary creation and a coin-age consumption transaction allows multiple improvements on Peercoin's protocol. It aligns coin creation with Proof-of-Work blocks, enables multi-signature minting (described in RFC-0003) and provides easily manageable limitations on the power of minters to make free transactions.

RFC—0003—MULTI-SIGNATURE MINTING (authored by Hrobeers)

An advantage of splitting the coinstake transaction into a monetary creation and a coin-age consumption transaction, as described in RFC-0002, allows the coin-age consumption transaction to be pre-signed off-line. In combination with multi-signature scripts, this could serve as an alternative to cold-minting.

On the 5th April 2017, PeerAssets Architect Peerchemist became the Project Leader of the Peercoin project. He received unanimous backing from the community and the core team. It had become his responsibility to keep a watchful eye on the cryptocurrency space by researching new technologies and being visionary. A more detailed description of the Project Leader role was given:

> "As part of the project leader's official duties, he will use the insight gained from this continuous research to help connect the dots and provide a vision and a plan of action for Peercoin's future. He will work directly with the development team, providing them with both the focus and direction necessary to lead Peercoin to success. Sunny King approves of Peerchemist in taking this official role and has offered him his full support. Sunny will of course continue his current role within the dev team as founder and lead developer of the Peercoin protocol."

The core Peercoin team had also been defined and now officially consisted of the following members and corresponding roles:

Sunny King (Peercoin Architect—Lead Protocol Developer)   Saeveritt—Developer

Peerchemist (Project Leader—PeerAssets Architect)   FuzzyBear—Developer

Sigmike—Core Protocol Developer   Backpacker69—Developer

Hrobeers—Core Protocol Developer   Nagalim—Core Member

Sentinelrv—Community Manager—Public Relations   Irritant—Core Member

Also on the 5th April 2017, the community was informed that the difficulty of mining Peercoin proof of work blocks had increased approximately four times (see chart below) since the beginning of March 2017. It reached a high over 2 billion for the first time. This meant that the annualised inflation rate of generated PPC was at its lowest level so far.

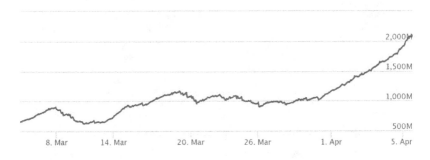

Other events which occurred during this period included:

- On the 30th January 2017, both Sentinelrv and Peerchemist (replacing kappamale) became administrators of the Peercoin Subreddit. Also, Jooize, CapR, Cybnate, Hrobeers and Nagalim all became moderators there.

- On the 3rd April 2017, the number of Peercoin Twitter followers surpassed 6,000 for the first time (439 in the past month alone).

- On the 5th April 2017, the total number of PPC generated to date surpassed 24,000,000 as soon as block number 294,525 was timestamped.

- On the 26th April 2017, the fiat price per PPC surpassed US$1 for the first time since 10th July 2015.

I.   CORE PEERCOIN WALLET CLIENT RETHEMED TO REFLECT REBRAND

II.   RFC-0004 PROPOSAL SUBMITTED ON 17TH MAY 2017

III.   HITBTC EXCHANGE INITIATED PPC TRADING ON 17TH AUGUST 2017

IV.   PEERCOIN FIFTH ANNIVERSARY ON 19TH AUGUST 2017

V.   PEERCOIN VERSION 0.6 PROTOCOL PROGRESSION DISCUSSED

12

VERSION 0.6
DEVELOPMENT

*"We decided to try something different with update #6
and record an audio interview introducing some members of the
development team and why they got involved with Peercoin"* - Sentinelrv

For the past couple of months, the Peercoin developers had been testing new code protocol (version 0.6) for eventual release. Sentinelrv informed the community, in late April 2017, that great progress was being made. In particular, the Peerunity community wallet client, which had been in use since the 30th May 2014, would no longer be supported after the version 0.6 wallet client software release. Work was underway to move all the feature functionalities from Peerunity to the core qt wallet client. Sentinelrv also posted:

> **"The migration of Peercoin to the Bitcoin v0.8 codebase has been successfully tested on testnet. The team is now discussing some protocol upgrades like porting over some newer Bitcoin OP codes such as OP_CHECKLOCKTIMEVERIFY."**

As always, members of the community were encouraged to stay informed about progress by visiting the Peercoin forum and other related social media channels.

As part of the ongoing transition, the graphical user interface (GUI) of the core qt wallet client was being rethemed to reflect the new PPC logo and colour scheme. Sentinelrv had taken the Peerunity community wallet design as the template for the updated theme. Sigmike was tasked with implementing the code designs into the client. What follows is a screenshot of the new design (compare to the GUI of the Peerunity wallet client on page 90).

"So how do you guys like the updated theme? It's in the same format as the old client, but all the colors/logos have been changed as well as it being brighter and simpler looking."

On the 4th May 2017, the price per PPC surpassed US$2 for the first time since the 23rd June 2014. What follows is a table of historical figures derived from www.coinmarketcap.com showing the ascent in prices:

	Low US$	Open US$	Close US$	High US$	Market Cap US$
2nd May 2017	1.18	1.23	1.25	1.27	29,990,826
3rd May 2017	1.22	1.25	1.42	1.47	34,290,849
4th May 2017	1.43	1.43	1.93	2.17	46,548,714

On the 17th May 2017, the fourth RFC protocol improvement proposal "Remove Transaction Timestamp" was created. It is summarised as:

> "Peercoin's transaction timestamp is not strictly needed by the protocol and can be arbitrarily chosen by the transactor with very little restrictions. The timestamp provides a small but unfair advantage to educated users and breaks compatibility with Bitcoin infrastructure. Removing the transaction timestamp facilitates broader adoption of the Peercoin blockchain by increasing the amount of compatible tools and enables the development of protocol improvements like <u>multi-signature minting</u>."

Since the 14th April 2017, funds were being raised for the realisation of the first token-issuance DAC built using PeerAssets. Five trusted members of the Peercoin team (Nagalim, mhps, Peerchemist, Saeveritt and Backpacker) were responsible for holding the funds within a multi-signature wallet address. Funding goals achieved were as follows:

- On the 19th April 2017, the minimum US$50,000 funding goal was met.

- On the 4th May 2017, over US$150,000 had been raised.

- On the 24th May 2017, the maximum US$250,000 had been raised.

Unfortunately, later in the year, the Indicium project fell through due to the sheer cost and complication of regulations. All funds raised were eventually paid back.

On the 27th June 2017, Sentinelrv informed the community that Peercoin version 0.6 was still under active development. It had been recently rebased to Bitcoin version 0.8.6 codebase. Additionally, it would implement the ability for users to opt -out of synchronised checkpoints and include OP_CHECKLOCKTIMEVERIFY. At the time, the developers were busy preparing to carry out a fork of the protocol on the testnet blockchain.

Before the Indicium project fell through, a visual representation of Indicium was unveiled on the 25th July 2017. It was designed by Lightning (the same person who designed the Peercoin logo back in July 2013). Sentinelrv was quoted as saying:

"A tip for some who are seeing it for the first time. The symbol can be viewed in 2D, but also 3D if you focus on the center. In 3D it can be seen as a cryptocurrency basket. The center is the opening. The leaf imagery on the bottom also connects it back to Peercoin/PeerAssets."

On the 17th August 2017, the cryptocurrency exchange HitBTC initiated PPC trading. Two trading markets (see below) were made available for users of the exchange to buy/sell PPC. Members of the community were happy to see a new PPC/USD trading pair, because BTC-e had recently closed down.

https://hitbtc.com/PPC-to-BTC
https://hitbtc.com/PPC-to-USDT

HitBTC has been providing traders the ability to buy and sell cryptocurrencies (such as Bitcoin, Ethereum and Litecoin) since early 2013.

Block #318,210 (Reward 0.41 PPC) August 19th 2017 2016 at 18:34:27 UTC

As shown above, block number 318,210 marked the time at which the Peercoin blockchain turned five years old. A total of 24,273,167.52 PPC had been generated since the first block was timestamped on the 19th August 2012. The annualised inflation rate stood at approximately 3.59% on this day.

On the 3rd September 2017, as an alternative way to update the community, the Peercoin team recorded an audio video. Sentinelrv, Peerchemist, Hrobeers, Nagalim, Saeveritt, and Sunny King via text, discussed current developments and future objectives. It was hosted by Intelliguy who hosted the Peercoin Fourth Anniversary Beyond Bitcoin Radio Show back in August 2016.

Besides introducing themselves and their respective roles within Peercoin, the team reported that Peercoin version 0.6 had already successfully passed multiple testing rounds. It was also the case that some fine tuning still had to be done before the official release.

Other events which occurred during this period included:

- On the 25th June 2017, the number of Peercoin Twitter followers surpassed 10,000 for the first time.

- On the 27th July 2017, the exchange BTC-e ceased operation. BTC-e had been the most liquid exchange for PPC trading over the last four years. This event impacted the price per PPC; hundreds of thousands of PPC were stolen and sold on the open cryptocurrency markets.

- On the 21st September 2017, BTC38 ceased PPC trading.

- On the 23rd September 2017, an infographic (see page 106) was published as a visual representation of what an ICO for PPC might have looked like.

I.   PUBLIC TESTING OF VERSION 0.6 BEGAN ON 6TH OCTOBER 2017

II.   PEERCOIN VERSION 0.6.0 RELEASED ON 25TH OCTOBER 2017

III.   RFC-0005 AND RFC-0006 IMPROVEMENT PROPOSALS SUBMITTED

IV.   PEERCOIN MARKET CAP SURPASSED US$100,000,000 AGAIN

V.   VERSION 0.6 SOFT FORK ACTIVATED ON 20TH DECEMBER 2017

13

VERSION 0.6 SOFT
FORK ACTIVATED

*"There is no deadline indeed, the fork will not activate if it isn't supported
by the network. Also running a v0.5 client will not fork you off the chain after
the fork activated. Your blocks will just get orphaned." -* Hrobeers

After months of code development and testing, Peercoin version 0.6 was ready for
public testing. On the 6th October 2017, the first release candidate (v0.6.0ppc.rc1)
was made available for technically minded people to test its functionality and
limitations. Project Leader Peerchemist announced that testing had begun:

**"Please note that experience with compiling and operating a Peercoin node
in developer-like environment is required to participate in this test. To assist
the developers with testing you must know how to compile the Peercoin
source-code and submit logs if you experience some problems.**

The Peercoin development team wished to, first of all, have a successful switch to
v0.6 protocol on testnet before releasing the full release for the Peercoin
blockchain. An upgraded Peercoin release candidate (v0.6.0ppc.rc2) was uploaded
to Github on the 19th October 2017.

On the 25th October 2017, Peercoin version 0.6.0 was released. It was the long awaited soft fork and first release from the new Peercoin development team. It marked the transition away from Peercoin being solely developed by Sunny King and Sigmike, although Sunny King had still greatly contributed to the recent code. It also marked the end of the Peerunity community wallet client. What follows are some of the code protocol changes version 0.6.0 introduced:

- Rebase to Bitcoin v0.8 codebase (leveldb backend).

- Allows wallet users to opt-out of checkpoints.

- Activates soft fork, at the earliest, on the 12th December 03:40 UTC if 90% of the last 1,000 proof of stake blocks come from the version 0.6 client.

Developer Hrobeers responded to those who questioned whether a deadline to upgrade to version 0.6.0 had been set. He was quoted as saying:

> "There is no deadline indeed, the fork will not activate if it isn't supported by the network. Also running a v0.5 client will not fork you off the chain after the fork activated. Your blocks will just get orphaned (you won't be able to produce blocks anymore)."

During November 2017, two more RFC protocol improvement proposals were submitted for the community to read and discuss. They were:

RFC-0005: Unspendable Zero Outputs (authored by Hrobeers)

> "Peercoin requires outputs to have a value of at least 0.01 PPC. It's unclear to the author why this value has been chosen, but it seems a reasonable dust prevention measure. However, there is one exception to this rule, 0 PPC outputs are allowed. Such zero-value outputs can have some useful applications, but an unfortunate side-effect is they take up memory in the node's UTXO table forever, increasing it's memory usage. This RFC proposes a solution that fixes this memory leak without changing the rules for output values."

RFC-0006: Remove Proof-of-Work Block Signature (authored by Hrobeers)

> "Peercoin blocks contain a block signature covering it's contents, as is required by the Proof-of-Stake algorithm. Unfortunately this block signature requirement has also bee imposed on Proof-of-Work blocks, while these don't strictly need the signature as the Proof-of-Work covers the entire block's content. This RFC proposes the removal of the requirement for a valid signature in Proof-of-Work blocks."

On the 29th November 2017, the fiat price per PPC surpassed US$4 for the first time since February 2014. Many other cryptocurrencies were also experiencing rallies. As shown immediately below, the Peercoin market capitalisation again surpassed US$100,000,000.

Date	PPC (US$)	PPC (BTC Sat)	Volume (US$)	Market Cap (US$)
29th November	4.10	37,741	9,319,240	100,241,502

For the community to monitor the percentage of wallets which had upgraded to version 0.6 protocol, a website at https://www.peercoinexplorer.net/forkwatch had been active. According to this website, the following thresholds were surpassed:

- On the 5th November 2017, soft fork v0.6 hit 10% adoption.

- On the 8th November 2017, soft fork v0.6 hit 25% adoption.

- On the 4th December 2017, soft fork v0.6 hit 50% adoption.

- On the 13th December 2017, soft fork v0.6 hit 75% adoption.

On the 20th December 2017, the Peercoin protocol code finally switched to version 0.6 at 06:15:08 UTC. The Peercoin team thanked everyone who had updated their wallet client software.

Going forward, there was much to discuss, consider and implement. Cold minting (an important security enhancement) and a Peercoin Foundation were being discussed:

Other events which occurred during this period included:

- On the 20th October 2017, the exchange Bitsane initiated PPC trading.

- On the 7th November 2017, Peercoin version 0.6.1 was released.

- On the 29th November 2017, Tux Exchange initiated PPC trading.

I.   ALL TIME 2017/18 HIGH PEERCOIN MARKET CAPITALISATIONS

II.   PEERCOIN VERSION 0.6.2 RELEASED ON 11TH MARCH 2018

III.   PEERCOIN DISCORD SERVER CREATED ON 3RD APRIL 2018

IV.   PEERCOIN VERSION 0.6.3 RELEASED ON 23RD APRIL 2018

V.   PEERCOIN PARTNERED WITH STAKEBOX ON 8TH MAY 2018

14

2017/2018 PEERCOIN
MARKET CAP RALLY

"Peercoin is the pioneer of Proof of Stake blockchain technology, currently operating efficiently at 1/4000th the amount of energy required to secure Bitcoin. Instead of being controlled by miners, it is collectively governed by its users, everyone who owns Peercoin."

At the beginning of 2017, the fiat price per PPC was approximately US$0.25 according to the www.coinmarketcap.com ranking website. On the 18th December 2017, following a sharp rally for one month, the price attained an all time 2017 high at US$6.83 per PPC.

Other cryptocurrencies were also experiencing bull runs during 2017. As shown by the table below, historical figures for Bitcoin, Ethereum and Peercoin, on the 18th December 2017, are recorded as follows:

	Low US$	Open US$	Close US$	High US$	Market Cap US$
Bitcoin	18,355	19,106	19,114	19,371	320,174,318,520
Ethereum	689.32	721.73	794.65	803.93	76,623,897,492
Peercoin	5.55	5.72	6.65	6.83	163,158,639

On the 13th January 2018, the US Dollar price per PPC attained its all time 2018 high. It reached at peak at US$9.92 at which the corresponding PPC market capitalisation is recorded at approximately US$243,699,680.

Date	PPC (US$)	PPC (BTC Sat)	Volume (US$)	Market Cap (US$)
13th January 2018	9.92	68,514	12,227,100	243,699,680

On the 13th February 2018, the Peercoin team released an updated PPC paper wallet generator. Members of the community are free to access the service via the https://paperwallet.peercoin.net address. Sentinelrv was quoted as saying:

> "The team would like to announce the release of a new Peercoin paper wallet address generator which was developed by @kazzkiq.
>
> The new generator can be found at https://paperwallet.peercoin.net and will act as a replacement for the wallet generator developed by FuzzyBear that has been in use for several years.
>
> The main focus for the new generator was achieving a simpler and more modern interface while also making it ligher so load time on mobile devices are shorter. The result is a generator that is simple, clean and 10x lighter than the nearest wallet generator. In addition, it works on both mobile and desktop."

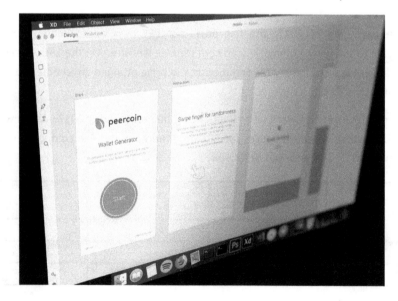

After three months of code testing on testnet, Peercoin version 0.6.2 was released on the 11th March 2018. As usual, the relevant download links were available from the https://github.com/peercoin/peercoin/releases/ address. It implemented multi-signature GUI dialog and other code bug fixes.

On the 3rd April 2018, Sentinelrv announced the launch of the Peercoin Discord channel to help Peercoin increase its user base. Other cryptocurrencies had also being utilising the communication platform to organise their discussions in different customised channels. Discord is compatible with functional desktop and mobile applications. Sentinelrv posted the following update:

> Discord has a large registered user base, making it is easy for existing users to join Peercoin's community simply by joining the server. This ease of access will increase participation in the community. Unlike Telegram which only has a single room, the Discord server supports multiple chat rooms dedicated to different topics. It also features voice servers where community members can talk to each other live."

https://discord.gg/XPxfwtG

Two events occurred on the 23rd April 2018:

- Peercoin version 0.6.3 was released. It fixed minor code bugs found in the previous version.

- A cryptocurrency exchange called Freiexchange initiated PPC trading.

On the 8th May 2018, Peercoin formed a partnership with StakeBox. It is a Pi Supply brand and a world leading distributor of Raspberry Pi mini computers. For the last three months, the Peercoin team had been working with StakeBox to create a piece of hardware for securely minting PPC (see images below).

In addition to people being able to purchase the staking device with PPC, there are several benefits to the partnership:

- Pi Supply actively market the staking devices they create. Therefore, more people become aware of Peercoin over time.

- The Peercoin Foundation (established on 14th May 2018) receives a fraction of the profits for each Peercoin StakeBox sold by Pi Supply.

- The Peercoin team pass updates to Pi Supply's repository, allowing for seamless automated updates of all StakeBox devices.

- Ultimately, the partnership is helping to grow the number of Peercoin nodes across the world, increasing the decentralisation, and hence the security, of the Peercoin network protocol.

Other events which occurred during this period included:

- On the 22nd December 2017, the Livecoin exchange initiated PPC trading.

- On the 24th January 2018, Sunny King announced that he had assumed a full time position as chief architect of a new project called VEE. He emphasised his continued care for Peercoin and Primecoin as well as congratulating ongoing code development by the Peercoin development team.

- On the 11th March 2018, an article titled "Peercoin Explained: The Proof of Stake Pioneer" was published on the https://bitfalls.com website. It was written by Dinko Vranjičić. Sentinelrv described it as well written and informative.

I.   **PEERCOIN FOUNDATION ESTABLISHED ON 14TH MAY 2018**

II.   **PEERCOIN LEDGER NANO S SUPPORT BEGAN ON 22ND MAY 2018**

III.   **PEERCOIN VERSION 0.6.4 RELEASED ON 5TH SEPTEMBER 2018**

IV.   **FIRST OFFICIAL PEERCOIN FOUNDATION BOARD MEETING**

V.   **BOTH RFC-0007 AND RFC-0008 ACCEPTED ON 5TH NOVEMBER 2018**

15

PEERCOIN FOUNDATION ESTABLISHED

"The Peercoin Foundation opened in May 2018 and was registered in the Netherlands. The Foundation allows for legal opportunities previously unavailable including partnerships and the further advancements of the Peercoin project." - Sentinelrv

For several years, prominent members of the Peercoin team had rejected the idea of forming a foundation due to it being considered as a form of centralisation. In May 2018, the team realised the benefits for establishing a recognised entity that would make future relationships possible in a constantly evolving cryptocurrency space. Key benefits of a foundation are:

- To provide Peercoin with legal representation. For example, it makes it possible to form legal partnerships with third parties.

- To legally collect donations from the community for financing ongoing development of the Peercoin ecosystem.

- To strengthen marketing efforts.

- To write up legally compliant documents for remaining active on exchanges.

On the 14th May 2018, Sentinelrv excitedly announced the official opening of the Peercoin Foundation. It had been registered in The Netherlands. On the same day, a Peercoin multi-signature wallet address was disclosed for anyone who wishes to fund the project. A description of the fund is as follows:

> "This is a general donation fund to be used to support the Peercoin project as a whole, not for any specific project within the Peercoin ecosystem. Any funds spent will be at the discretion of the foundation's board members."

p92W3t7YkKfQEPDb7cG9jQ6iMh7cpKLvwK

On the 16th May 2018, three RFC protocol improvement proposals were submitted to the relevant Github repository website. RFC-0009 did exist, but was pulled. They are summarised as follows:

RFC-0007: Round Transaction Fees Up To 0.001 (authored by Backpacker69)

Currently transaction fees are rounded up to nearest 1 hundredth of PPC and any small transaction under 1024 bytes must pay at least 0.01 PPC to be included in the block. Transaction of 1025 bytes must pay at least 0.02 PPC to be considered etc.

It is proposed to have fee rounding changed in such way that all transactions will pay exact proportional to size fee for the right to be included in the block, at unchanged rate of 0.01 PPC per kilobyte, with 0.001 PPC minimum.

Effectively, transaction up to 102 bytes will pay minimal fee of 0.001 PPC. Transactions of bigger size will pay unrounded fee proportional to their byte size.

RFC-0008: Increase OP_RETURN Size Limit (authored by Backpacker69)

Increase OP_RETURN size limit to 256 bytes.

RFC-0010: MIN_FEE as Standardness Rule (authored by Peerchemist)

Make MIN_FEE variable a standardness rule, which defines whether transactions gets relayed, and not a hardcoded protocol rule.

Sentinelrv encouraged technically minded community members to contribute to all the active RFCs at https://github.com/peercoin/rfcs/issues. It was important to discuss and review the benefits and flaws of each RFC before the release of Peercoin version 0.7 in the future.

On the 22nd May 2018, a company that develops security and infrastructure solutions for cryptocurrencies called Ledger officially announced support for Peercoin. It became possible to securely store PPC on a Ledger Nano S hardware wallet. Peercoin was also added to the Ledger Manager App.

"Ledger was launched in 2014 by eight experts with complementary backgrounds in embedded security, cryptocurrencies and entrepreneurship, united around the idea of creating secure solutions for blockchain applications. We are have over 130 employees in Paris, Vierzon and San Francisco."

"Ledger Nano S is a hardware wallet, based on robust safety features for storing cryptographic assets and securing digital payments. It connect to any computer (USB) and embeds a secure OLED display to double-check each transaction with a single tap on its side buttons."

Over the following weeks, and into the summer, some members of the community perceived Peercoin progress to be sluggish. The Peercoin team issued a response on the 4th July 2018 to counteract the uncertainty:

"Some of you are completely underestimating the amount of time it takes to update Peercoin to where it needs to be. We are currently making great progress and the recent foundation has helped speed certain things up. We are currently in a bear market, so this is the perfect time to get important work done to be ready for when market sentiment changes again."

On the 19th August 2018, the Peercoin blockchain had been operational for six years as soon as block number 382,333 (see below) was timestamped. The Peercoin team admitted that the anniversary had flown by unnoticed, but again acknowledged Peercoin as the pioneer of proof of stake. Also, the number of PPC had grown by 2.65% over the past year.

Block #382,333 (Reward 0.06 PPC) August 19th 2018 at 18:25:13 UTC

On the 5th September 2018, Peerchemist announced that Peercoin version 0.6.4 had been released. He described it as a "bugfixes and polish" release. It introduced small fixes including multiple GUI improvements and new DNS seed nodes.

To provide a proper guide to introduce people to Peercoin, Sentinelrv had been very busy, for about five months, researching and writing an educational section for the upcoming new Peercoin website. What began as material covering the security and economics of Peercoin soon turned into something more in depth.

On the 10th September 2018, Sentinelrv published the material (Peercoin University) for the community to review. Unlike the Design Paper published by Sunny King, it would become the ultimate beginner's guide for understanding Peercoin. Peerchemist was thanked for his help during the research phase.

On the 25th September 2018, two days after the first Peercoin Foundation board meeting occurred, an update was posted. Sentinelrv announced that several people had been hired (see page 127) and also posted the following:

> "Besides the new hires, the first major resolution that was voted on was about the Foundation itself and whether it will support any forks of Peercoin. The board has voted that the Foundation will only support the blockchain network that runs the code which resides on https://github.com/peercoin/peercoin
>
> Another item for discussion was about whether the Foundation should support second layer technologies that are built on top of Peercoin with the goal of extending use cases and functionality. While the board is interested in improving the Peercoin ecosystem with additional supporting layers, it was felt by many board members that for now we should primarily focus on developing the core protocol. Second layer protocols may find more support in the future once the Foundation attains higher levels of funding, but they would need to be evaluated on a case by case basis."

On the 25th September 2018, the Peercoin Foundation announced that four people had joined the Peercoin team:

- EvgenijM86 had been hired as a core developer. He was formerly the Lead Developer for Emercoin. He had recently worked on the rebase of Peercoin to Bitcoin Core version 0.16.3 (prepares for SegWit and Lightning Network).

- Solomon Lederer was voted in as treasurer (volunteer role).

- Backpacker had been hired as a full-time developer. He was already familiar with the Peercoin codebase. He became the administrator of the official Peercoin Github repository website where he contributes to, and resolves issues with, code development.

- Buckkets had been hired as the PPC Community Manager. He administers Peercoin related social media channels including Discord and Telegram. He is also responsible for reaching out to third parties. Buckkets had recently set up the partnership with Blockfolio Signal.

On the 31st October 2018, Peerchemist announced Project Perpera. It is an implementation of the PeerAssets DataAudit code protocol. A brief description of the project was posted:

> "Perpera is a library written in TypeScript and aims to cater to the needs of future web-based applications and development/power user focused CLI tools.
>
> The main purpose of this protocol is the embedding of arbitrary documents into the blockchain (proof-of-existence) and the ability to revise said documents. In this aspect (support for revisions), this protocol is different than similar protocols which are already in use."
>
> https://github.com/peercoin/perpera

On the 5th November 2018, RFC-0007 and RFC-0008 (see page 124) were accepted in the upcoming Peercoin version 0.7 release. The Peercoin development team reiterated the motivation behind these protocol improvement proposals as being to ease and increase the adoption of the blockchain.

Peercoin Foundation Established

Other events which occurred during this period included:

- On the 18th May 2018, the packaging sleeve for the new Peercoin StakeBox was unveiled (see adjacent page).

- On the 4th June 2018, funds residing in deemed abandoned projects on the peer4commit website were transferred to the Peercoin Foundation multisig wallet address p92W3t7YkKfQEPDb7cG9jQ6iMh7cpKLvwK.

- On the 7th September 2018, an improved version of the Peercoin paper wallet generator at https://paperwallet.peercoin.net/ went live.

- On the 14th September 2018, the Kompler exchange initiated PPC trading.

- On the 17th September 2018, the Coin Switch service began to offer its users the ability to buy/sell PPC.

- On the 21st September 2018, Peercoin was added to Blockfolio Signal.

- On the 26th September 2018, Magnum Wallet integrated Peercoin.

- On the 16th October 2018, the total number of PPC surpassed 25,000,000 as soon as block number 392,455 was timestamped.

- On the 26th October 2018, Peercoin went live on Delta Direct. It is a platform via which the community can receive team updates.

What's Inside?

 Raspberry Pi 3

 Peercoin case

 Power supply

 16GB SD card with Peercoin software

 HDMI cable

Earn Peercoins

The Peercoin network is secured through an efficient validation process called proof of stake minting. Minters hold peercoins in their wallets and over time they produce new blocks for the network, which earns them new peercoins.

Efficient Minting

The Peercoin StakeBox runs on a Raspberry Pi 3, allowing you to participate in the minting process 24 hours a day, 7 days a week at minimal energy cost. Just load it with peercoins and let it sit and mint for you in the background.

Portable & Secure

The Peercoin StakeBox is small and compact, making it easy to move. Minting on a dedicated StakeBox rather than your everyday computer also means you are less exposed to viruses and hackers, increasing the security of your peercoins.

What is Peercoin?

Peercoin is the world's first efficient and sustainable blockchain technology. The core function of Peercoin is providing a decentralized and censorship resistant public blockchain for the world to use. Peercoin acts as a secure base layer for the future blockchain connected world.

Pioneer of Proof of Stake

Released in 2012, Peercoin was the first cryptocurrency to invent and introduce proof of stake consensus to the world.

Distributed Store of Value

The Peercoin blockchain is designed for storing your wealth in decentralized form where it's secure from external threats.

Direct User Governance

Coin holders have the power to directly influence the network and its rules through PoS minting, ensuring decentralization.

Cost Efficient Security

Peercoin provides an energy efficient network that is secured at low cost, ensuring long-term security & sustainability.

I.   PEERCOIN RFC-0011 PROPOSED ON 9TH NOVEMBER 2018

II.   BRAND NEW OFFICIAL PEERCOIN WEBSITE WENT LIVE

III.   PEERCOIN VERSION 0.7.0 RELEASED ON 22ND JANUARY 2019

IV.   PEERCOIN VERSION 0.7.1 RELEASED ON 17TH FEBRUARY 2019

V.   PEERCOIN BLOCKCHAIN HARD FORKED ON 12TH MARCH 2019

16

VERSION 0.7
PROTOCOL SWITCH

"Buying Peercoin is like investing in a mining rig that never becomes
obsolete. Minting blocks uses time as a scarce resource rather
than computational power, any ordinary computer can be used."

For most of the year, the Peercoin development team had been discussing which features to include in the next code protocol upgrade. Peercoin version 0.7 had reached the stage at which testing on the Peercoin testnet blockchain began on the 8th November 2018. A hard fork of the Peercoin blockchain would be required to implement changes (including the accepted RFC-0007 and RFC-0008 proposals).

On the 9th November 2018, the eleventh RFC protocol improvement proposal titled "Proof-of-Stake Inflation Adjustment" was submitted by Nagalim:

> **"While PoS inflation can currently be up to 1% per year, in reality only a**
> **fraction of the existing coins participate in the minting process. This RFC will**
> **seek to continuously adjust the PoS block reward such that PoS inflation approximates**
> **to 1%/year on average, no matter how much PoS participation there is. In general, this**
> **RFC will look into the intricacies of tying a block reward to the total supply, as well**
> **as how to safely implement a fluctuating block reward."**

After the submission of RFC-0011 to the relevant Github repository website, it became possible for skilled coders to contribute to its development. Increasing the Peercoin proof of stake block rewards will likely increase staker participation, and hence increase the security of the Peercoin blockchain.

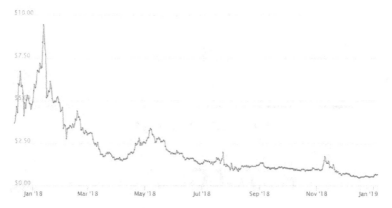

Throughout most of the year, most cryptocurrency market capitalisations experienced bear market territory. The US Dollar fiat price per PPC decreased more than 90% from the all time 2018 high (see chart above) on the 13th January 2018. Despite the downward trend, the Peercoin team reaffirmed their dedication towards being as ambitious and visionary as possible.

What follows is a table of historical data related to Peercoin derived from www.coinmarketcap.com

	Low US$	Open US$	Close US$	High US$	Market Cap US$
13th January	8.06	8.07	9.05	9.92	222,504,662
13th February	3.43	3.64	3.47	3.66	85,370,907
13th April	1.83	1.86	1.88	1.96	46,400,416
13th June	1.46	1.53	1.55	1.55	38,420,876
13th August	1.16	2.29	1.17	2.60	29,236,469
13th October	0.872359	0.900898	0.897033	0.932262	22,422,858
13th December	0.520762	0.558015	0.541341	0.578628	13,583,266

On the 1st January 2019, Sunny King wished the community a happy new year. He posted a statement on https://talk.peercoin.net about plans for 2019:

> "First of all, congratulations to the Peercoin team for getting the v0.7 release into good shape! During the final review process it was discovered that some minor fixes still need to be completed so the planned v0.7 release date and protocol switch date will be adjusted accordingly. Keep an eye on the team's upcoming announcements.
>
> In 2019 the Peercoin team plans on finishing up development work v0.8, which will feature Peercoin's rebase to Bitcoin-core 0.16.3. Significant progress has already been made on this work and the completion of coding may be right around the corner. Also, something else we are excited about is the redesign of peercoin.net, which is currently under construction and expected to be released sometime in the new year!
>
> In the last couple years, Proof-of-Stake Consensus has steadily gained popularity over Proof-of-Work Consensus. It is evident that the trend will continue in the coming years due to the efficiency and scalability advantages. Peercoin will continue to showcase the technology advantage and innovations it brings to the crypto world.
>
> Happy New Year to all Peercoin supporters and crypto fans!
> Have fun!"

After many months of designing, researching and content writing, a revamped official Peercoin website went live on the 7th January 2019. The community had been looking forward to it for a while. Brand new sections were included:

- New documentation located at https://docs.peercoin.net provides important links and useful information. New users are able to gain access to tutorial guides.

- The long awaited Peercoin University educational resource was uploaded to https://university.peercoin.net where new community members can learn what Peercoin is. It begins by explaining what blockchain is and how its underlying technology can be used to enhance security of individual and business day-to-day activities.

Sentinelrv described the revamped website (see top of page 134) as a basis on which to build as time goes by. He also admitted that all resources were still in the editing phase, but were sufficient for publication.

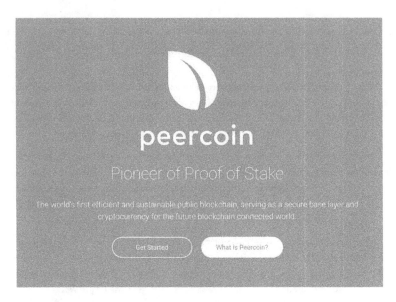

During January 2019, two cryptocurrency exchanges initiated PPC trading:

- On the 8th January 2019, the BitTurk exchange based in Turkey initiated the PPC/TRY trading pair.

- On the 15th January 2019, the Amsterdex exchange began to offer its users the ability to buy/sell PPC.

On the 22nd January 2019, following on from meticulous, thorough and successful testing, Peercoin version 0.7.0 was released. Users had to upgrade their wallet client software before the scheduled hard fork (to activate the protocol code changes) on the 12th March 2019 at 12:00 UTC. It implemented changes from RFC-0007 and RFC-0008 as planned. Sentinelrv posted a summary:

> "Both protocol changes improve the core economic parameters of Peercoin. Changing the granulation of the transaction fee is about keeping the core principle of 0.01 Peercoin per kB of data, but not forcing the user to round it up to 0.01 and overpay for the service.
>
> Increasing the max size of transaction data field (OP_RETURN) allows for more complex payloads while using the PeerAssets and Perpera protocols, while exploiting the same natural anti-spam feature of the Peercoin blockchain, that is that data cost 0.01 Peercoin per kB and naturally limits the amount of blockchain "bloat"."

As anticipated when Peercoin version 0.7.0 was released, another upgrade (version 0.7.1) was released on the 17th February 2019. It introduced changes to the wallet client design theme. Brighter colours (lighter green, lighter grey and white) were chosen to match the new Peercoin branding. Despite its release, the scheduled hard fork deadline date remained the 12th March 2019.

On the 12th March 2019, the Peercoin blockchain successfully hard forked and smoothly switched to version 0.7 code protocol. Block number 419,368 marked the time at which the protocol changes activated (see below).

Block #419,368 (Reward PPC) March 12th 2019 at 12:13:58 AM UTC

Going forward, the Peercoin development team are testing version 0.8 code protocol on the testnet blockchain. It will update the Peercoin blockchain to code based upon Bitcoin Core codebase v0.16.3 with several cherry-picks from v0.17.1.

APPENDIX

Vitalik Buterin Interviewed Sunny King on 8th August 2013

Sunny King:	Nice to see you Vitalik!
Sunny King:	I am still amazed by your quality technical articles on Bitcoin Magazine.
Vitalik Buterin:	well thank you!
Vitalik Buterin:	always glad to get feedback so I know what to write more of
Sunny King:	and to absorb all the materials on primecoin within one day and wrote such nice long article
FuzzyBear:	yup avid reader here and love your articles as well :)
Sunny King:	that's an amazing feat
Vitalik Buterin:	not many people toe that middle ground line between writing and advanced comp-sci I suppose
Vitalik Buterin:	Bitcoin (and coins in general) are like that though; brings lots of things together
Vitalik Buterin:	anyway, I'm a big fan of what you guys are doing here too
Vitalik Buterin:	I think you're probably the single most original altcoin developers out there
Vitalik Buterin:	well, there's Ripple too, but in bitcoin terms they're a large corporation
FuzzyBear:	yup sunny has my vote by a mile
Sunny King:	Thanks really appreciate it
Vitalik Buterin:	so, question 1
Vitalik Buterin:	Who are you? What's your background? Are you Sunny King in real life, or is that just an internet identity?
Sunny King:	Yeah it's a pen identity, similar to Satoshi's tradition I guess
Vitalik Buterin:	any hints as to what you do outside of altcoins?
twobits:	Ripple is not really a coin
Vitalik Buterin:	@twobits Ripple is not really a coin: I throw it in there because I think its idea of "consensus" is a serious competitor to PoW/PoS, and brilliant if it can be made to work. It has problems though, no doubt about that

Sunny King:	Although I didn't really take that extreme measures so at least some of my friends know I am doing this
Sunny King:	The main reason is that I hope if political climate turns worse in the next couple years that I could still buy some time to make a bit more contributions
Vitalik Buterin:	do you think it will?
Sunny King:	I did some c programming before and currently work mostly on cryptocurrency
Sunny King:	possibly since events this year already confirmed my concerns (and satoshi's)
Sunny King:	but I think primecoin could also help to bring another positive argument for cryptocurrency
Vitalik Buterin:	yep, I agree
Vitalik Buterin:	I'm staying in Spain right now, and it's interesting how the culture here is much more egalitarian/social oriented than, say, the US would tolerate. Among those who don't like Bitcoin, the two major arguments are (1) early adopter unfairness and (2) mining is wasteful
Vitalik Buterin:	you've done quite well in solving (2)
Vitalik Buterin:	do you have any opinion on the early adopter issue?
Sunny King:	if so I think the market is now trying to wrestle with (1) with all these altcoins
Vitalik Buterin:	how so?
Sunny King:	from my point of view I don't think early adopter is an 'issue' per se with bitcoin
Sunny King:	just like the gold miners and 'hoarders' are not an issue with gold
Sunny King:	although it does appear to me that the market force behind cryptocurrency is different from precious metals
Sunny King:	in the old commodity money gold eventually does dominate
Sunny King:	but it seems much harder for bitcoin to sustain such dominance in cryptocurrency

Vitalik Buterin:	why do you say that?
Sunny King:	one observation is that lots of miners and investors are looking at new altcoins hoping to strike it right, even if it is a pure clone without anything new
Vitalik Buterin:	yeah, I'm finding the interest in pure clones very strange
Sunny King:	I guess this has to do with the early adopter issue that you mentioned
Vitalik Buterin:	why do you think people care about them?
Sunny King:	That also perplexes me a bit but I think the market is treating the currencies as competing companies, you know like stocks
Sunny King:	But I also found some other deeper elements at work that may undermine bitcoin's dominance eventually
Sunny King:	this has something to do with bitcoin's scarcity and the specialization of mining hardware
Sunny King:	which I think underscores the rise of litecoin since last year
Sunny King:	this I have described a bit in my design paper of primecoin,
Sunny King:	basically I think bitcoin's overall security against 51% attack would drop in the future against other competing currencies
Vitalik Buterin:	because the block reward would keep going down
Vitalik Buterin:	right
Sunny King:	this could become a basis for it to lose dominance in the long term
Sunny King:	although this is still speculation and the process likely is still years away
Vitalik Buterin:	? isn't primecoin theoretically subject to the same effects?
Vitalik Buterin:	it's block reward will likely decrease quadratically (assuming Moore's Law) and not exponentially, so it will be slower.
Sunny King:	but as a designer I need to be aware of the possibilities so this is part of the reasons for introducing primecoin
Vitalik Buterin:	but a hundred years down the line they'll both be very low
Sunny King:	I think designing for a hundred years is unrealistic, but I do look at 20 years and possibly beyond

Sunny King:	so primecoin tries to weaken the scarcity model a bit to compensate for a sustained mining market and higher security
Sunny King:	bitcoin has a stronger scarcity model than gold, but I think having something closer to gold is good enough
Sunny King:	so both ppcoin and primecoin take this approach with their scarcity
Vitalik Buterin:	the inverse quadratic rule, right
Sunny King:	yeah for primecoin block value is 999/difficulty^2
Vitalik Buterin:	? why not just 999/block number^2 ?
Sunny King:	so when moore's law hit the wall it would become constant generation but still low inflation
Vitalik Buterin:	with some fudge factor near the beginning
Sunny King:	this is because I don't like to guess a fixed schedule
Sunny King:	so I'd rather for market to decide when it should become more scarce
Sunny King:	so it's design as more miners and better hardware/algorithm would mean lower production
Sunny King:	the timing is then determined by market
Vitalik Buterin:	well, it's determined by the market in the exact opposite way that, say, gold supply is determined by the market
Vitalik Buterin:	gold: more miners/better algorithm -> more supply
Vitalik Buterin:	is there any conscious reason behind doing it that way?
Sunny King:	not exactly, it actually still resembles gold
Vitalik Buterin:	primecoin: more miners/better algorithm -> less supply
Sunny King:	more supply is temporary, just like say the 2nd week of primecoin there are a lot more production than normal
Vitalik Buterin:	well, that was the lag in difficulty adjustment
Vitalik Buterin:	which is a different issue
Sunny King:	but for gold mining it just appears on a longer time scale so it's less obvious
Vitalik Buterin:	now, though, my estimate of the final supply of xpm got adjusted down by 50-100 mil after that big spike

Sunny King:	it's not really different they are connected, for gold mining you are just moving future production to now, it's just over many years so not obvious
Vitalik Buterin:	hmm, that's an interesting argument actually
Sunny King:	whereas bitcoin/primecoin adjust difficulty in a week or two
Vitalik Buterin:	I personally have always wanted a coin with deliberately slow difficulty adjustment (eg. Timespan of 3-12 months); seems like that would also approximate gold in a different way
Sunny King:	that wouldn't work well because block spacing would be destroyed
Vitalik Buterin:	true
Sunny King:	for example several altcoins got stuck at high difficulty after the first few days
Vitalik Buterin:	maybe make difficulty adjustment rapid but increase the reward for some time instead...
Vitalik Buterin:	there are many idea
Sunny King:	it's generally agreed now that bitcoin's 2-week adjustment schedule is not suitable for a new altcoin
Vitalik Buterin:	the problem there wasn't the 2-week schedule, so much as the 2016 block schedule
Vitalik Buterin:	if your diff is 10x too high, that
Vitalik Buterin:	is 20 weeks
Vitalik Buterin:	anyway, I saw you made an interesting post a month ago on the ppcointalk forums
Vitalik Buterin:	[LINK] ...sg1715
Sunny King:	yeah this problem was actually hit by namecoin, the first altcoin so they developed merge mining for this
Sunny King:	that's strategic reason for the design of primecoin
Vitalik Buterin:	talking about what your strategy with Primecoin was
Vitalik Buterin:	so you think that the proof-of-* mechanism is essentially the major part of Bitcoin that can be improved, and want the community to focus more on looking for and promoting solid alternatives

Sunny King:	of course first I had to have the idea that primecoin could technically work, but then I am looking for reasons why we should run two coins do primecoin can be made
Vitalik Buterin:	is that accurate?
Sunny King:	so that's primecoin strategic reason
Sunny King:	So from late last year litecoin has spectacular rise that made me think about why and the competitive position of ppcoin vs litecoin
Sunny King:	it's possible that market would favour something simpler than ppcoin in the shorter term e.g. next couple years
Sunny King:	so primecoin would be a good candidate in the sense that it's designed to have most litecoin's so-called advantages over bitcoin
Sunny King:	yet still being innovative and brings new ideas
Vitalik Buterin:	in terms of new ideas
Vitalik Buterin:	I saw somewhere, whether in the source code or the discussions, that you were working on some kind of improved checkpointing system for ppcoin and/or primecoin
Vitalik Buterin:	something not quite centralized
Sunny King:	yeah its already in primecoin, it's an updated version of ppcoin's checkpointing system
Sunny King:	even ppcoin's checkpoint is not meant to stay centralised forever
Sunny King:	and it's going to work similarly in ppcoin in the future as well
Vitalik Buterin:	so how does this new checkpointing system work?
Sunny King:	basically developers can broadcast a checkpoint to the network, and if an user turns on the checkpoint enforcement in the node then it would follow the block chain fork of the checkpoint
Sunny King:	this means that if the majority of network enforces the checkpoints then developer has power to thwart a sustained 51% attack

Sunny King:	while the network is turning into a temporary centralization mode
Sunny King:	although there are built-in checks to ensure even in the checkpoint mode developers cannot arbitrarily abuse this power
Vitalik Buterin:	how did the system work before?
Sunny King:	in ppcoin right noew the checkpoints are enforced by default so users have no say in whether to follow it or nor
Vitalik Buterin:	ah, okay, so hardcoded into the software essentially
Sunny King:	yeah but it will be switched over in the future
Vitalik Buterin:	>although there are built-in checks to ensure even in the checkpoint mode developers cannot arbitrarily abuse this power< - what kinds of built-in checks are you talking about?
Sunny King:	the system is designed because threat of 51% attack is real with altcoins
Sunny King:	there is a consistency check with checkpoints
Sunny King:	meaning that developers cannot issue conflicting checkpoints and force double-spending on the network
Sunny King:	for example, say developer checkpoint is issued on a block with 6-confirmatons, then you can treat the transaction confirmed earlier than the checkpoint is safe
Sunny King:	he cannot invalidate that checkpoint and ask the network to go into another block chain fork
Vitalik Buterin:	what if a developer sends two conflicting checkpoints to two parts of the network at the same time?
Vitalik Buterin:	so half picks up one first, half picks up the other
Sunny King:	that would cause the network to fork and requires manual intervention like restarting or upgrading client
Vitalik Buterin:	okay, makes sense
Vitalik Buterin:	if it was perfect, you would just use it instead of the pow/pos in the first place

Sunny King: in primecoin user could also then ignore checkpoint and just follow the fork with more work

Sunny King: checkpoint is a temporary centralisation defence against 51%, not on the same level as PoW or PoS

Vitalik Buterin: is it a jsonrpc command to do this, or are you planning on adding a GUI as well?

Sunny King: oh the Qt now has a debug window which can do all the rpc commands

Vitalik Buterin: right, forgot about that

Vitalik Buterin: so what are the next steps / near-term goals in primecoin development at this point?

Sunny King: but if needed we could ass it as an option-setting

Sunny King: I think infrastructure and marketing would be the top priority for primecoin, more exchange support, mining pools and so on

Sunny King: the team is also expanded quite a bit so primecoin shouldn't lag behind while I work on ppcoin v0.4

Vitalik Buterin: are you planning on integrating the latest btc features eventually? (eg. Payment protocol)

Sunny King: sure both primecoin and ppcoin should keep reasonably up-t—date with bitcoin features

Sunny King: right now primecoin is ahead of ppcoin in this regard

Vitalik Buterin: what is ppcoin 0.4 going to have? The advanced checkpointing system?

Sunny King: It's mainly a refresh to bitcoin v0.8 features, but there could also be some adjustment on certain protocols

Sunny King: the checkpoint would be adjusted a bit also but it won't be as decentralized as primecoin yet

Sunny King: btw ppcoin now has numerous copies in the market and I have now stopped counting them

Vitalik Buterin: yeah it seems like proof of stake is slowly becoming more accepted. Also, as far as proofs go, in the ppcoin paper you mentioned a third possibility

Sunny King:	just past several weeks saw at least three copies released in china and went into speculative frenzy
Vitalik Buterin:	"proof of excellence"
Vitalik Buterin:	could you elaborate a bit more on that idea?
Sunny King:	it's a concept although there is no concrete designs around this concept
Sunny King:	it's based on that a tournament result of some games is difficult to forge
Sunny King:	for example you cannot go to a tennis tournament to win prizes without having some serious skills
Vitalik Buterin:	so a coin might have some kind of internal AI tournament?
Vitalik Buterin:	best programmers win and get to mine some blocks
Sunny King:	so it's a possible candidate to replace the functions of proof-of-work
Sunny King:	Yeah that's the idea
Sunny King:	It doesn't have to be AI it can be done between humans as well
Vitalik Buterin:	true
Vitalik Buterin:	although coins don't really have a way of distinguishing between human players and bots
Vitalik Buterin:	the only challenge I know of that humans are better at is Go
Sunny King:	right and most games AI can play better than humans
Sunny King:	I actually looked at Go and I think even for that the network would be dominated by bots
Sunny King:	because there is already very goof Go AI and very few pro level Go players
Vitalik Buterin:	yeah
Vitalik Buterin:	and ideally you do want the system to be somewhat egalitarian as otherwise one party might get 51%
Vitalik Buterin:	whoever has the best Go algorithm
Vitalik Buterin:	that's probably the hard part about implementing it

Sunny King: that's one of its issues because its distribution is a lot more concentrated than proof-of-work

Sunny King: Vitalik do you sense a general change of attitude toward altcoins?

Vitalik Buterin: yes, I can feel it

Sunny King: I am actually quite surprised that Bitcoin Magazine carried primecoin the first day since my impression earlier was that there was no interest

Vitalik Buterin: six months ago, altcoins were almost irrelevant

Sunny King: and only time I saw anything mentioned was ripple

Vitalik Buterin: consider this

Vitalik Buterin: teleport yourself to Dec 2008

Vitalik Buterin: simultaneously release bitcoin and primecoin

Vitalik Buterin: which one do you think people will like more?

Vitalik Buterin: I think primecoin might be the first one to actually beat Bitcoin on that test

Vitalik Buterin: litecoin was nice, but scrypt is overcomplicated

Vitalik Buterin: ppcoin is, as you said, too complex

Vitalik Buterin: Ripple is also too complex

Vitalik Buterin: it can only survive because Bitcoin came first to ease people into the idea of cryptocurrency

Vitalik Buterin: I think people are slowly realizing that there are still serious improvements to the core idea of cryptocurrency that can be made

Vitalik Buterin: and at the same time the community got big enough to support them all

Vitalik Buterin: here in Calafou (place in Spain), ever since I introduced the locals to Primecoin people have been thinking, since we have one example of a useful PoW, what else can we do?

Sunny King: yeah I got a few messages regarding ideas of other useful work types

Vitalik Buterin: we came up with the idea of an AI challenge-based coin independently too (although no progress toward anything practical)

Vitalik Buterin: what do you think are some promising directions?

Sunny King: that's what I hope primecoin would inspire other designers to do

Sunny King: I am not sure, there seems quite a bit demand to monetize F@H, and I hard Pande is looking at the matter seriously

Sunny King: But it's not easy to come up with a proper decentralized design

Sunny King: The things is, the innovative systems are quite costly to develop, and the market doesn't seem to reward original ideas that well in the altcoin arena

Vitalik Buterin: F@H?

Vitalik Buterin: ah, folding at home

Sunny King: So I have seen a lot of such attempts fail because of lack of funding for development

Vitalik Buterin: yeah, the problem there is how you make it uncheatbale

Vitalik Buterin: alright, anything else you wanted to talk about?

Sunny King: that's a good chat thanks a lot Vitalik

Sunny King: yeah we've covered quite a bit

Vitalik Buterin: alright, thank you too!

Sunny King: Looking forward to chatting with you again in the future :)

PeercoinTalk Community Interview with Sunny King #1 on 19th October 2013

JustaBitofTime: 1. What existing impediments do you think keeps PPC from being the absolute perfectly designed crypto—and are there ways to change it to get it there? (Excelsior)

Sunny King: I don't think there could be a perfect all encompassing cryptocurrency that dominates all. Bitcoin is the breakthroughof a grand experiment. From architect point of view, you can try to design for excellence, but in a sense we are all still learning in the grand experiment. Proof-of-stake is a young approach I am sure quite a bit of improvements can be made. I am generally not as strict regarding hard fork upgrade so we can do a bit if needed.

JustaBitofTime: I read in your Bitcoin Magazine interview about 'Proof of Excellence' has any further thoughts went into that approach?

wantrepreneur: Do you expect potential xpm hardware ASICs require much larger breakthrough in cpu-computing-> more so than SHA-256?

Sunny King: Not much because I don't yet find a game suitable enough as a basis for the idea. Most games are dominated by AI so there would be a lot of complaints of unfairness.

JustaBitofTime: I'll go ahead and number to make it easier to follow for those just joining us.

JustaBitofTime: 2. What is your one-year plan and mid-term roadmap that implements your strategy? (Mhps)

irritant: I think one of the advantages of XPM is that it can be mined by everyone, if that is true also on the long term it would make it grow more organically, without ASIC race madness, do you think this is important for cryptocurrency?

Sunny King: @wantrepreneur Not sure, although Primecoin is not designed to hamper ASIC. So I think maybe a large performance improvement can be achieved through ASIC. That's actually a huge milestone forxpm if that even materialize. On the other hand, mining algorithm can improvequite a bit too so the field of xpm mining is very cheap.

Sunny King: @irritant I don't see ASIC development necessarily bad for the currency, it's one of xpm's major contribution to technology ifthat ever happens.

irritant: Yes true.

ivanlabrie: Sunny, are there any plans to implement pos blocks in xpm, or any other way of preventing 51% attacks?

irritant: I see ASICs to centralise mining with bitcoin.

Sunny King: @2. The main strategy of the team has already be shown, ppc/xpm would be our combo attack in the market. The twocurrencies are designed very differently, each with its own unique innovations, improving our overall competitiveness in the market. For ppc the next step is tobring it up to bitcoin v0.8 features in v0.4, xpm would get some protocol tighteningin v0.2. I hope the cold-locked feature can be implemented next in ppc. Cooperation with the service providers in the industry is also an important goal. Idon't want to overpromise here but I think we are actually one of the most activedev team around.

irritant: But I 'm not sure if it will become a problem.

JustaBitofTime: 3. Do you have a contingency plan to keep the currencies going should (god-forbid) something happen to you? (Excelsior)

Sunny King: @irritant I don't know, it seems to be bitcoin mining scene won't change all that much from the gpu days, there are always big players and small players.

Sunny King: @Excelsior That's something on my plate. For ppc scott can be my backup, but he hasn't been very active since ppc's release. For xpm mikael has been doing a good job. I would hope more talents would join the community so there are more capable hands that can take over the responsibilities during emergency situations. So the expansion of the core dev team is also an important goal.

JustaBitofTime: 3.5. Could tell us a bit about the full development team and is this a full time job for you (xpm/ppc)?

wantrepreneur: And to expand on #3, could the code eventually be developed to no longer rely on anyone?

Sunny King: Core dev of ppc is me and scott, xpm is me, mikael, jh and mtrlt.

Sunny King: Yeah almost full time right now. It's part of my goal that I could achieve self-sufficiency in the cryptocurrency market, so I can continue to commit most of my time to development work.

JustaBitofTime: 4. The main thing I want to see Sunny address in detail is the accusation that proof of stake is setup like central banking, where the rich get richer and the poor get poorer. Certain people have problems with the fact that those who own the most coins will get the most newly minted coins. (Sentinelrv)

Sunny King: That's only core dev which maintains the client codebase. of course many of you have made great contribution are also part of the development team.

JustaBitofTime: Sunny: I know you've answered number 4 before in other posts/ interviews... just curious if anything has changed.

irritant: What motivated you to start all this, was it some flaws you saw in bitcoin, or is it more... that you want to change the world, make it better place, more fair?

Sunny King: @wantrepreneur, That's not very realistic as continued development/maintenance is a key requirement for the success of a cryptocurrency.

JustaBitofTime: @wantrepreneur: Sounds like a key backup on the PPC is an upcoming priority.

Sunny King: @Sentinelrv 4. For argument's sake let's assume that proof-of-stake minting is free from the risk of hacked wallet. So the argument boils down to whether holding the currency should deserve some compensation. It's a similar debate to whether some interest on money is deserved. From my point of view I think interest by itself is not the problem, who wants to lend money without interest? As a free market phenomenon I think interest has some legitimate roots, so it's very much separate from central banking, which is an entirely different animal based on statism ideologies.

Sunny King: @Sentinelrv 4. The proof-of-stake minting provides a service to the ppc network, so why shouldn't those who provide the service receive some compensation? The rich and the poor are treated the same here, both can provide proof-of-stake minting, and rate of income is proportional to their holding. So you can say that the rich get richer, and the poor also get richer, at the same rate, so long as they both try to provide the service to the community. Meanwhile, those who transact in the network with high velocity pay the security cost via low inflation.

JustaBitofTime: 5. What legacy do you wish to leave through your Peercoin experience? (MeBeingAwesome)

Sunny King: @MeBeingAwesome 5. @irritant I cherish my work in cryptocurrency very much and I think they are the best works of my career. Not only from a technology and innovation point of view, but also from political and spiritual point of view, I think cryptocurrency movement is one of the most important event in our time, that humanity now owns a very potent weapon against tyranny. So I am very proud to be able to participate in the movement.

irritant: I wish I could do more, maybe I will learn some day (programming etc).

JustaBitofTime: 5.5. You mentioned a weapon against tyranny. Isn't that the reason you're so careful with your identity?

JustaBitofTime: 6. About how many more weeks until PPC v0.4 comes out? What will be the new features? (Alertness)

irritant: On irc the imposter mentioned " @fontas: Absolutely. The team is currently looking at ways to implement matlab/simulink derived distributed simulations." I guess it is not true right? (too bad)

Sunny King: Right although the movement is entirely peaceful through free market principles. I am not too worried though I believe what we do is morally good even if it's banned legally in the future.

Sunny King: @irritant yeah that's just some guy's joke.

Sentinelrv: Just want to confirm, there was a Sunny King imposter on IRC? I heard he said he worked in the aerospace industry and people thought it was NASA. This is not true right?

JustaBitofTime: Sunny: While you work through question 6, I'll post the next 2 for you.

Sunny King: @Alertness 6. Merge with bitcoin v0.8 is more work then I thought. Meanwhile I am evaluating whether to provide the cold-locked transaction feature in v0.4, as it has become a higher priority item. But v0.4 would get most bitcoin v0.8 features for sure. I think it's at least still several weeks away.

JustaBitofTime: 6.5. The new Bitcoin 0.9 is going to implement some nice things like an independent RPC client binary, and fix some centralization problems. Not to mention the other stuff that we have missed. I suggest we merge with the 0.9 release, and go from there. (Super3)

JustaBitofTime: 7. Will proof-of-stake minting be made more easy to do or even automated? (Matt608)

JustaBitofTime: We're at question 7 of 12. Sunny has agreed to 45 minutes (11 left) … if he wants to continue past the 45 min to finish, great… if not, we'll get those answered in a follow-up.

Sunny King: @Super3 I haven't looked at bitcoin v0.9 yet so it's hard to say when it would be included. We need some buffer time for new bitcoin code to stabilize also.

JustaBitofTime: 8. Have you looked at Zerocoin? If so, do you see that or something similar as a direction for PPC? (JustaBitofTime)

Sunny King: @Matt608 7. Proof-of-stake minting is automated if you are not using wallet encryption. If you use encrypted wallet you can turn it on via debug window console in v0.4. In the future gui element may be added to further simplify the procedure.

JustaBitofTime: "In the future gui element may be added to further simplify the procedure." +1

Excelsior: +1

Sunny King: @JustaBitofTime 8. I haven't studied zerocoin in detail but it appears there were serious concerns regarding its usability (in terms of computation and storage requirements) and certain centralization issue. I feel zerocoin is a highly complex system and could be too expensive for the problem at hand.

JustaBitofTime: 9. Can you explain how the ppc checkpoint system works by community consensus in the event of persistent 51% attack on proof-of-stake or other emergencies, and how that even though the checkpoints are currently centralized, this is not synonymous with ppc itself being centralized. Explain how there is no centralized control over changing ppc, but that in order to revert back to a checkpoint it still takes community consensus. (Alertness)

JustaBitofTime: 10. Folks in the other community have been bitching about the check point. Rumor has it is to be removed by the of year (PPC). Is that right ? What is the reason behind such time frame ? What about XPM? (Romerun)

Sunny King: @JustaBitofTime 8. There are other more cost-effective approach to privacy in my opinion. For example in bitcoin privacy is compromised mainly through the fact that coins belonging to different keys owned by the same user are often combined in the same transaction when spending. This allows blockchain analysis to easily establish what set of keys are from the same user. In bitcoin client combining of inputs from different addressed is automatic, however if this is left to the user to decide then privacy can be much stronger. I call this approach 'avatar mode', where each key/address is considered an avatar. So the client would not automatically spend coins belonging to different avatars in the same transaction. So you would have a number of avatar addresses to manage. Of course this doesn't guarantee absolute privacy but could be quite an improvement practically speaking.

JustaBitofTime: 9 + 10 blend

JustaBitofTime: Ah... avatar mode was one of my questions for future interviews.

irritant: Ahh I see, avatar mode is coincontrol, avatar mode +1

Sunny King: @alertness @romerun XPM is already decentralized. The checkpoints in xpm is like the alert message, clients listen to them but does not enforce the checkpoint by default. Users have the choice to enable the enforcement of checkpoint, but it's a conscious choice users must take. This means the developer responsible for the checkpoint must gain community consensus before using them, developer cannot arbitrarily force a block chain reorganization onto the users. Generally speaking the checkpoint feature should not be used without 51% attack emergency.

JustaBitofTime: And finally 11 and 12.

JustaBitofTime: 11. As of PrimeCoin PR, it would be really nice to have an article published in one of recognized popular science, or non-peer-reviewed science journals such as New Scientist, Science Illustrated, Scientific American etc. (CryptoBeggar)

JustaBitofTime: #12 was already answered (full time job)

Sunny King: @alertness @romerun The risk of 51% denial-of-service attack on block chain is real, especially to a smaller network such as xpm. In fact I wouldn't exclude such possibility to even bitcoin. Of course such an attack on bitcoin would likely not come from an individual due to the resource required. But it's irresponsible to say that's not possible. Just imagine what would happen if bitcoin stops processing transactions for a few days. The advanced checkpoint feature in xpm is specifically designed to deal with this situation. Yes the network would turn into quasi centralized mode by community consensus, however that's obviously a lot better than admitting defeat and giving up.

Sunny King: @CryptoBeggar 11. I am very happy to see experts such as John joining this effort, so I am confident that it would happen at some point. As our marketing improves and users keep spreading the words the interest from science journal and other media would definitely increase. I feel this something not only beneficial to primecoin, but it also bring another positive element to cryptocurrency, so the mainstream have more focus on the good things cryptocurrency can bring to the society.

PeercoinTalk Community Interview with Sunny King #2 on 24th October 2013

Sunny King: Hi all.

JustaBitofTime: Hey Sunny, nice to have you with us. Are you ready to get started?

Sunny King: Yes John I'm ready.

JustaBitofTime: Coolbeans94 wanted to know about Peercoin's long term approach, he asks "27. Is its design more for long-term security and sustainability? How does that relate to Bitcoin's longterm vision? (Coolbeans94)"

Sunny King: @Coolbeans 94. Both PPC and XPM are designed to last. PPC is designed with energy efficiency, XPM is designed with energy multiuse. Bitcoin has a long term uncertainty as to whether transaction fees can sustain good enough level of security. Before that the main concern is how to balance transaction volume and transaction fee levels. Currently I get the feeling that bitcoin developers favor very low transaction fees and very high transaction volume, to be competitive against centralized systems (paypal, visa, mastercard etc) in terms of transaction volume, to the point of sacrificing decentralization. This also brings major uncertainties to bitcoin's future.

Sunny King: @Coolbeans 94. From my point of view, I think the cryptocurrency movement needs at least one 'backbone' currency, or more, that maintains high degree of decentralization, maintains high level of security, but not necessarily providing high volume of transactions. Thinking of savings accounts and gold coins, you don't transact them at high velocity but they form the backbone of the monetary systems.

Sunny King: @Coolbeans 94. Pure proof-of-work systems such as bitcoin is not 100% suitable for this task. This is because transaction fee is not a reliable incentive to sustain network security. If the mining generation amount is kept constant (there have been several such attempts in altcoins) it would work better security-wise but then it would also significantly weaken the scarcity property of the currency. XPM's inflation model is designed in such a way that it could serve as backbone currency better than bitcoin if needed, because it could maintain high security reliably for longer, with reasonably good scarcity property as well. Of course that's only from architect's point of view, whether or not it would be chosen by the market is a whole different matter.

JustaBitofTime: Along those lines the community wanted to know ""If the tax fees are to remain fixed at 0.01 and Peercoin becomes widely adopted, (Thus a sharp rise in value) the fees could become too much for microtransactions. What would happen in this case? What solutions do you imagine to get around the microtransaction issue?"

Sunny King: @Coolbeans 94. PPC is designed to serve even better as a backbone currency. The proof-of-stake technology in PPC is not only energy efficient; it also maintains high level of security without relying on transaction fee. Thus PPC could be safely designed with strong scarcity property yet serving well as backbone currency.

Sunny King: @Coolbeans 94. Both PPC and XPM use protocol enforced transaction fees, which reflects my preference that high transaction volume is discouraged in favor of serving as backbone currencies.

JustaBitofTime: Speaking of security, there's often quite a bit of debate surrounding the PPC vs XPM checkpointing. 27.5 Will checkpoints be optional like they are in XPM in the next client version?

Sunny King: @transaction fees: Right now if we are talking about micropayments in the US$1 range, both PPC and XPM still handle them with much lower overhead than credit card network. In the long term micropayments should be provided by centralized providers, or a less decentralized network optimized for high capacity transaction processing.

Sunny King: @transaction fees: On the other hand there is no promise that minimum transaction fee wouldn't be adjusted. If processing capacity of personal computers continues to advance at the current pace, both max block size and minimum transaction fee could very well be adjusted at some point. However I do take a very cautious approach to adjusting transaction fees, as opposed to bitcoin devs. The impact to the fitness of the currency as a backbone currency is of great concerns to me.

Sunny King: @checkpoint: Decentralization of PPC checkpoint is currently planned to begin in v0.5. It would be a gradual process.

JustaBitofTime: I can tell you from my own Libertarian leaning, being able to add some layer of anonymous transactions is important to me. 47. Can you tell us more about 'sendtoaddressfrom' and Avatar mode? Will this be released in the next client version? (JustaBitofTime)

Sunny King: @JustaBitofTime Yeah this is still at conceptual stage. It shares some similarity to coin control. However from user point of view I'd like them to think in terms of avatars instead of addresses and coins, it's simpler and better for privacy.

Sunny King: The main rule is that in avatar mode the client doesn't automatically assemble coins from different avatars into the same transaction.

Sunny King: But it can still do so within an avatar.

JustaBitofTime: One of the challenges the Peercoin community faces is breaking down all the technical nuances of the coin. Alertness asks "60. Could you please explain exactly how the level of PoW and PoS difficulty is calculated? (Alertness)"

Sunny King: So you probably need to specify which avatar the money should come from in a send.

Sunny King: I would wait to see how coin control is introduced in bitcoin first. If bitcoin implements similar concepts first that would be nice too.

Sunny King: @Alertness For simplicity we can think of the difficulty adjustment of PoW and PoS blocks independent of each other. Basically it uses some technique called 'exponential moving' to keep the block spacing relatively constant. It adjusts on every block and smoother than bitcoin's adjustment, responding to change of network hash rate much faster than bitcoin, but at the same time not too fast to make difficulty manipulation exploits difficult.

Sunny King: @Alertness PoS blocks have a constant 10-minute spacing target. PoW blocks have a variable spacing target, between 10-minute and 2-hour, but on average it's about 30-minute when PoS block spacing is close to the 10-minute target. This serves to reduce the variation of block spacing.

JustaBitofTime: Along those lines, 60.5 Could you please spend some time talking about the environmental impact of Bitcoin vs Peercoin now and then in the future? (JustaBitofTime)

Sunny King: @JustaBitofTime I don't like to paint bitcoin in a negative picture because it's indeed a brilliant system with high integrity and reasonably good inflation design. High energy consumption is only a minor blemish. To say that it's gold 2.0 I think is quite reasonable.

Sunny King: But if we can solve one of the issues with gold and gold 2.0, their environmental impact, that would be very nice, wouldn't it? We all want to live on a cleaner and happier earth, right? So we should take this task more seriously and PPC provides a possible solution.

Sunny King: On the other hand we should also respect other people's free will. For example we should not force other people to not mine bitcoin or participate in distributed computing projects, because of the environmental cost. So XPM complements the goal here as it produces additional scientific value from the consumed energy. So people who like to mine cryptocurrency for whatever reason have a better choice to mine, to get more benefit out of the mining activity and environmental cost.

JustaBitofTime: For our non-technical users, how does PoS factor into the environmental impact? In other words, 1 friend is mining Bitcoin and the other is mining Peercoin. How does that look now and how does it look in 1 year?

Sunny King: Currently PPC market cap is still small, so the effect is still small. If PPC becomes as successful as BTC, then the energy saving would be significant, and more and more so as difficulty rises.

JustaBitofTime: As difficulty rises, what is the net effect? I feel this is an area that many new to the coin have trouble making the connection.

Sunny King: A caveat here is that the energy consumption on bitcoin mining might drop in the long term as well, due to lack of incentive in mining. However this would drop bitcoin's security level.

JustaBitofTime: You spoke about producing additional scientific value from consumed energy with XPM. 55. What are your thoughts about F@H? Do you see a place for it in crypto coins?

Sunny King: Difficulty increase in PPC reduces inflation rate, which also reduces the energy consumption. This is assuming market capitalization stays the same.

Sunny King: It's hard to say, I am not an expert in protein folding algorithms but I can imagine it would be hard to completely decentralize. There has been a proposal of a less decentralized solution whereas traditional hashing provides network security and half of the minting, whereas folding computation provides the other half of the minting using the existing centralized distributed computing network. This approach is not limited to F@H though, people are also thinking about other networks such as BOINC.

Sunny King: The problem with this system is whether trust is required on the centralized distributed computing network to not abuse the system and counterfeit. Without solving such problems it's not a serious currency system in my opinion, but on the other hand we do see existing systems in operation with centralized minting, such as DVC and FRC. So this type of systems definitely has some niche in the market.

JustaBitofTime: Shifting gears here, Jimmy asks "Q1 New: When will the development team release the official ppcoin specification? (Jimmy) Clarification "We got the paper last year, but we need a protocol specification detail similar to **https://en.bitcoin.it/wiki/ Protocol specification**, especially for POS and the integration of POW with POS. The specification is important to developers and the general users who are interested in ppcoin."

Sunny King: @Jimmy There is no set plans for this yet. If the demand is strong I could look into getting a summary of difference between bitcoin protocol spec and ppcoin protocol spec.

JustaBitofTime: Between 2 different coins, you obviously have your hands full. Romerun asks "Last interview sunny say if he somehow disappears Scott will fill in. But up till now we don't really know who he is, or how much commitment of him to the project / etc. There could be the issue of impostor too, so it would be benefit to the community to clear this up. And wouldn't it be better to have a few more key devs to PPC."

JustaBitofTime: My understanding was Scott was capable of filling in, however, has not worked on PPC recently?

Sunny King: That's right. For some reason Scott isn't as motivated as I am. I also look forward to having more developers with ppc, right now I think xpm team is in good shape, quite a number of people are working on xpm miners which requires a good understanding of the innerworkings of primecoin.

Sunny King: So I think as our community grows there will be more talents showing up. I am still pounding scott to be actively involved as well.

JustaBitofTime: As your development team expands for XPM, Muto asks "35. Do you plan to release another currency? (Muto)"

Sunny King: @Muto 35. No such plan right now. I have recently turned down a few invitations to work on other currency projects due to my responsibility in PPC and XPM. I am committed to further improve PPC and XPM's competitiveness in the market.

JustaBitofTime: Speaking of competitiveness in the market, Romerun would like to know "What are the development priorities/future features of PPC/XMP in Sunny's mind? online wallet? ppc-blockchain.info? etc."

JustaBitofTime: I understand marketing and overall community development/involvement is a big part of the overall plan.

Sunny King: I have touched a few things last week I think, there are other things I have in mind but don't wish to talk about yet. I am constantly evaluating market situation to figure out what's the best features to compete in the market.

JustaBitofTime: Let's change it up again 8. Who are your business and personal heroes? (MeBeingAwesome)

Sunny King: As to services and apps I usually leave those to the market to support. If I were to be involved in a service somehow I think it needs to have profit potential.

Sunny King: And not divert too much of my resources and time.

Sunny King: @MeBEingAwesome Right now I am in the business of cryptocurrency As to my heroes, I think Satoshi qualifies as one. We know that before bitcoin came into existence, several pioneers in the digital currency world have made sacrifices, such as Douglass Jackson the founder of e-gold, Bernard von NotHaus the founder of Liberty Dollar, among many others. These efforts are part of the same movement to decentralize the control of money, from potentially rising oppressive governments. Gold was demonetized to mainly facilitate centralized power, that gives governments power to do a lot more damage, to do whatever they want. Through history we can see the corruption of morality of governments, for example, in the 1860's US governement still had the integrity to return to gold standard after civil war, while in the 1930's it no longer had such integrity after an economic depression. Not only that, it developed audacity to blame the depression on gold. It's very difficult to restore morality of governments.

Sunny King: The cryptocurrency movement, arising from the lessons of e-gold and liberty dollar, gives people a powerful tool to peacefully return to the principle of limited government. We all thank Satoshi whose brilliant mind and effort enabled this movement. Of course there are a lot more things going on in the societies outside cryptocurrency world, to preserve mankind's freedom, to elevate mankind's morality and spirituality, so there are many heroes around us.

JustaBitofTime: I completely respect your desire to remain anonymous. If the code is open, that should speak for itself. With that being said, there are people that claim you might be someone involved with the Satoshi team early on. Can you speak to that rumor? Also, did you have any involvement with Satoshi directly?

Sunny King: I wish I were as that would have made me very rich I am also curious to who Satoshi really is, what led him to such great achievement. But on the other hand I also wish him a peaceful life not having to endure such hardships like NotHaus.

JustaBitofTime: For those not familiar with NotHaus, please look into Liberty Dollar.

JustaBitofTime: On the flipside, D5000 has a question about a worst-case scenario. "44. What mechanism prevents PPC to collapse in a worst-case-scenario, e.g. a year-long strong bear market with steadily dropping hashrate, increasing mining rewards and higher inflation? (D5000)"

JustaBitofTime: (Note to community: We have Sunny for about 30 more minutes, I want to make sure you have time to ask a question I might not have covered)

Sunny King: @D5000 Practically there is a ceiling of inflation. Even though block reward would be higher when exchange rate drops lower, the extent to which this could occur is quite limited. For example, the first block of PPC (August 2012) is at difficulty 256, now PPC's difficulty is at 5 million. Even if exchange rate drops 100 times, the inflation rate would only increase say from 15% annual to 50% annual, still on a similar level to litecoin. So there is a ceiling of inflation rate that keeps getting lowered by Moore's Law. It's safe to say that in the worst case PPC's inflation would not exceed LTC's inflation for the next two years, most likely stay much lower than LTC. In the long term Moore's Law dominates the inflation model in PPC and XPM, over the fluctuations caused by market adoption and exchange rate. I use Moore's Law loosely here, inclusive of the effect of mining algorithm advances and the performance gain due to the transition from software mining to hardware mining.

JustaBitofTime: Q2 New: Is ppcoin less anonymous than PoW coin? If you solo mine your own coin on POW and use it, it's untraceable. I wonder if coin mined with POS contains the origin of the stake mining it, thereby can be traced. (Romerun) **http://www.peercointalk.org/inde...=585.0**

Sunny King: @Romerun The default minter in ppcoin client always keep the stake on the same address where it comes from. So yes it can be traced back on the same address, but it doesn't reveal much additional information with respect to privacy.

JustaBitofTime: Q4 New: What would be useful, and I'll see if I can find some figures, is to compare the power consumption of the Bitcoin network with future predictions with the Peercoin network on PoW/PoS and then also the current payment services providers network (for example, the power of the DCs that Visa/Mastercard/Amex run to process transactions)." (Nox-)

Sunny King: Some group did a paper a while back that attemps to analyze the energy consumption of bitcoin network I think. Although I feel they have a negative agenda there. This cost of bitcoin may very well be worthwhile compared to traditional centralized systems. But with more efficient systems such as PPC, bitcoin could face a bit competitive pressure.

JustaBitofTime: Sunny: I have a final question after Q4 New and then we'll open it up to any further community questions for the reminder of our time. Again, we sincerely appreciate you taking the time. It shows a lot of character supporting this community and its initiatives.

JustaBitofTime: What is the best way for media to contact you? Do you do phone interviews? What are the best times etc...

Sunny King: @Nox- To compare the energy consumptions, we would need to assume the systems are at similar capitalizations, and for PPC there needs to be an approximate curve of difficulty (maybe based on Moore's Law). One probable also make some assumption about bitcoin's future difficulty growth. It's not very reliable but I think it's doable for rough illustration purpose.

Sunny King: Right now I can only do online chat interviews or through email.

CoinDesk Interview with Sunny King and the Peercoin Team on 14th July 2016

Pre-Meeting Before CoinDesk Interview

Sunny King:	hi guys :)
hrobeers:	Nice to be with you in a chat room ;)
saeveritt:	Hey Sunny
hrobeers:	So how is this meeting organised?
Sunny King:	Sentinelrv thanks for organising
Sunny King:	Sentinelrv what's the agenda today?
saeveritt:	So do we know if Jacob has a specific set of questions or will it be a more of an open interview?
Sentinelrv:	Before we start...
Sentinelrv:	I was talking over with everybody here and we believe that it might be best to hold regular chats with you like this from now on. Would you be open to that?
Sentinelrv:	Everyone here consists of the most knowledgeable and active members of Peercointalk, so it would be great to regularly discuss the future of the network.
Sunny King:	sure absolutely
peerchemist:	I will take over for a minute
peerchemist:	so agenda here is to prepare Sunny for the new "official story" about Peercoin, so he could relay it to the interviewer
Sunny King:	okay :)
Sunny King:	I am all ears now
peerchemist:	so Sunny it is imperative that you now take the chance to mention why has PPC kept PoW—and what PoW means for us
peerchemist:	PoW is our market maker, just like it is for Litecoin and others
peerchemist:	it is VERY important to us
peerchemist:	and now changes in Btc are reflecting on our supply, so it is important to explain why and how

saeveritt: It seems that Jacob, the interviewer, approached the community looking to write a story focusing on the after affects of the BTC halving. Since it was mainly a non-event for most crypto Peercoin has the opportunity to show its market adaptability in comparison to others.

peerchemist: saeveritt, please link that graph to sunny

saeveritt: Emphasizing the importance of letting the market decide when to reduce supply rather than waiting an arbitrary X amount of blocks for reward reduction is something we should highlight.

peerchemist: https://plot.ly/~embeddedthought/49.embed11

peerchemist: here it is

saeveritt: Ok you got it already, thanks.

peerchemist: Sunny, do you see it?

Sunny King: yes

peerchemist: do you see how "leftovers" from Btc mining will reduce our supply and bring us closer to true PoS. PPC PoW is "pegged" to Bitcoin mining industry, as that industry bring more and more potent mining gear—stronger will Peercoin be

saeveritt: Yes. As long as BTC building the sha-256 mining infrastructure, PPC will continue to climb in difficulty and reduce supply. Since the BTC halving we've seen a coinbase reward drop of ~18%

Sunny King: who made the graph?

hrobeers: Important to note is that it lowers the maintenance cost of the network.

saeveritt: I made the graph. It uses simple curve fitting projections and I

peerchemist: this could theoretically make Peercoin take over the mining industry from Bitcoin sometime in the future. Once could also say that Peercoin "leaches of" a part of Bitcoin wealth each Bitcoin halving

Sunny King: nice. Peerchemist, this you got it, but only if peercoin becomes competitive vs bitcoin

peerchemist:	and thanks to PoS, we don't depend on miners for anything but distribution. We have "outsourced" distribution—but not the security
Sentinelrv:	Sunny, was it your intention for it to happen this way ever since you created Peercoin?
Sunny King:	it's also one of the reasons merge mining is not considered
hrobeers:	correct
Sunny King:	I don't say this much but be a small chance that ppc may pass btc in mining power. Merge mining would not allow this to happen
peerchemist:	yup, merge mining would be an "exit pump" for big holders. Coin would die shortly after
saeviritt:	True and it would only have temporary benefit of increased difficulty and decreased new supply to the market. Would not be optimal in the longterm as new supply to market helps harden rising price floor
hrobeers:	A nice extra of PoS is that it simplifies blockchain innovations. As everyone (holding ppc) had power to mint blocks, experimentation with non-standard transactions is easier
saeveritt:	Has anyone noticed that when there is a local peak in PPC PoW minted per day that the subsequent following days result in a price increase?
peerchemist:	I don't follow PPC market that closely, you are probably only trader who is deep into PPC I know
peerchemist:	so do we make fun of Ethereum now?
Sunny King:	whats wrong with Ethereum?
peerchemist:	just this clusterfuck with hard fork
saeveritt:	Have you seen Ethereum Classic is trading now?
peerchemist:	a part of community decided to keep the old chain
peerchemist:	now they are 51% PoW attacking each other, that is trying
peerchemist:	it is really really messy
hrobeers:	hahaa

peerchemist:	greed really deforms people, makes them monsters
hrobeers:	that's what I see popping around on Twitter :)
peerchemist:	manipulators on Poloniex are having one big party
Sunny King:	I thought Vitalik is in full control?
hrobeers:	where is Vitalik? Classic or hardfork?
peerchemist:	hardfork naturally, with the greedy ones, the "investors"
hrobeers:	:)
peerchemist:	Sunny I told you Ethereum is going the wrong way last time we spoke, and there it is now
Sunny King:	remind me why you think it's on the wrong way?
peerchemist:	private interest over the what is right and what is wrong
Sunny King:	isn't this occurrence due to complexity alone? oh
peerchemist:	immutability of the blockchain is what makes it so special
peerchemist:	they have disregarded that
peerchemist:	so why do they have the blockchain? to sell tokens it seems
peerchemist:	it will resolve itself eventually, those with principles will lose as they have less money
saeveritt:	I agree that the hardfork shouldn't have been forced the way is was. They had a deadline to do it by in order to prevent the DAO hacker from being able to withdrawal ETH from the contract. It was rushed and not everyone supported bailing out the DAO in this way.
Sunny King:	so why are ppl stay with classic?
hrobeers:	yep, history is controlled by a select group. Exactly why some people don't like the checkpoints, however it seems like checkpoints are irrelevant, people didn't expect that.
peerchemist:	because classic is saying "we will not alter history—ever"
peerchemist:	this is what I was warning a few times, that time will come when people will seek public and free blockchain—free from minority influence by big money. Peercoin is damn good position to be exactly that chain
Sunny King:	probably tougher than that. PoS can be bought as well

peerchemist: that is why we have continual PoW :)

hrobeers: good point

hrobeers: but in the end, everything can be bought

Sunny King: I see your points though, it would be ideal to not allow capital to gain too much control over protocol

hrobeers: That's indeed a good position to take these days

Sentinelrv: We've got almost 20 minutes left before it's supposed to start. Was there anymore interview preparation that we needed to go through? Or would you like to continue on the current path of discussion?

hrobeers: Let's try to sum up some of the conclusions already

saeveritt: Yeah, I see most 100% PoS coins with IPO's as something currently hyped. In the long-term contrinual distribution through PoW will show to harden the network in terms of decentralisation and network security. I wish we knew if Jacob has a specific agenda for the interview or if it's more of an open discussion

hrobeers: 1) Peercoin benefits from bitcoin's halving by the increased PoW hashrate, reducing ppc's operational cost by having a dynamic coinbase reward.

hrobeers: 2) PoW/PoS hybrid decentralises the network as much as possible. Buying the network (ref. Ethereum) becomes extremely expensive and complicated.

Sentinelrv: hrobeers, what is your definition of operational cost in #1?

hrobeers: network cost ~=PoW/PoS coinbase reward, outflux of value

Sunny King: it's not really cost, but a way to distribute the coins

hrobeers: it is a cost when used to pay for mining equipment

hrobeers: that cost is covered by the entire network

Sunny King: ok I guess you can say that, what I mean is it is not used for security of the network

hrobeers: oh but that doesn't matter

Sunny King: right

hrobeers: it's a cost covered by the network, someone pays that

hrobeers: our inflation decreases when hashing power rises, which means that our operational cost is going down. This way we can maintain a healthy network without a huge influx of money, like is needed for bitcoin, Ethereum and alike

hrobeers: it is not equal to the coinbase rewards but it scales with them

saeveritt: in terms of operational costs shouldn't only pos be considered since PoW isn't vital to operational security. If we were to compare with bitcoin and Ethereum, it would be the physical PoW infrastructure vs. virtual mining in PoS

hrobeers: 3) The decentralisation makes it possible for everyone to mint a block from time to time. This simplifies experimentation with non-standard txns on the network. This helps innovation.

hrobeers: no PoW is also part of operational cost, as it forces miners to sell ppc to buy mining resources. This is a cost by pushing the coins value down.

Sentinelrv: Jacob said he's currently talking to his editor and then he'll be on.

saeveritt: Also there is consistent incentive to secure the network in terms of the ~1% minting reward. There are other PoS networks that rely on fee structure as incentive. With NXT, almost all transactions are done off chain and on exchanges so incentive to secure to secure the network is dependent on fee volume. It's not reliable and that's why they need Ardor.

hrobeers: good point. I make it conclusion 4

saeveritt: increase on chain transactions to provide incentive to secure network other than protecting investment. Seems like supply stagnation sets when coins are being recycled between the major holders

hrobeers: these are the conclusions so far, you guys agree? Anything missing?

hrobeers: 1) Peercoin benefits from bitcoin's halving by the increased PoW hashrate, reducing ppc's operational cost by having a dynamic coinbase reward.

hrobeers: 2) PoW/PoS hybrid decentralises the network as much as possible. Buying the network (ref. Ethereum) becomes extremely expensive and complicated.

hrobeers: 3) The decentralisation makes it possible for everyone to mint a block from time to time. This simplifies experimentations with non-standard transactions.

hrobeers: 4) There is consistent incentive to secure the network in terms of the ~1% minting reward. There are other PoS networks that rely on fee structure as incentive. With NXT, almost all transactions are done off chain and on exchanges so incentive to secure the network is dependent on fee volume. It's not reliable and that's why they need Ardor.

saeveritt: Just to be specific, make sure to make point 1) say difficulty rather than hashrate

hrobeers: ok

saeveritt: Perhaps let him view this too? https://plot.ly/~embeddedthought/49.embed11

peerchemist: he should see that yes

hrobeers: I'll add it to my list :)

saeveritt: :)

Sunny King: maybe one of you guys should present the mining aspect

hrobeers: I'll make a gist of it

Sunny King: the mining rate curve was designed with Moore's Law in mind

peerchemist: now mention that if asked

Sunny King: but if price rises, the effect is similar

CoinDesk Interview with Sunny King and the Peercoin Team on 14th July 2016

CoinDesk Interview

JayCoDon:	Hey everyone—Jacob from CoinDesk here.
Sunny King:	Hi Jacob
Sunny King:	Welcome
saeveritt:	Hey Jacob
JayCoDon:	How are things?
Sentinelrv:	Hey
Sunny King:	Good we were just having fun here
JayCoDon:	You guys meet in here often?
Sunny King:	It's our meeting channel
Sunny King:	yeah sometimes
Sentinelrv:	Jacob, I know the meeting is with Sunny, but do you mind if others respond to questions as well. Everyone has a lot of knowledge about Peercoin here.
JayCoDon:	That's fine. I'll just need to know who they are and what their role with Peercoin is.
hrobeers:	Ok, we'll introduce ourselves first?
Sentinelrv:	Go ahead.
JayCoDon:	Sure.
Sentinelrv:	I'm pretty much the community manager and operate our social media channels. Others here have a lot more knowledge on the mining aspects than I do, which is why brought them into this.
hrobeers:	I'm hrobeers a developer that recently discovered peercoin. I've been helping peerchemist with his PeerAsset project and am developing a modular thin client wallet called PeerKeeper for an integrated experience.
hrobeers:	I made some small contributions to the official ppcoin client developed by Sunny

hrobeers:	https://github.com/hrobeers/ & https://twitter.com/hrobeers
peerchemist:	I am peerchemist, a developer of Peerbox. Inventor of PeerAssets and pretty much an all rounder when it comes internal stuff like help with marketing, educating newbies (like hrobeers) and theoretizing about blockchain and crypto in general
Sunny King:	hrobeers being modest, the peerkeeper is like a new generation wallet for peercoin
JayCoDon:	Likely very necessary for user adoption
peerchemist:	yep, PeerKeeper is the fanciest take on wallet tech since Electrum
hrobeers:	:) thanks guys
hrobeers:	Important to mention is that peerchemists Peerbox, is a full node meant for Raspberry Pi's, is crucial for the unmatched decentralisation that ppc has.
hrobeers:	Running a full node that mints (PoS mining) is a very simple process for any peercoin supporter thanks to Peerbox.
JayCoDon:	Alright, so to confirm: Sentinelrv is community manager, hrobeers is a developer that has made a next gen wallet for peercoin; peerchemist is a dev that created Peerbox, PeerAssets, and does some community and marketing. And Sunny King is the creator of peercoin. That sound about right?
saeveritt:	JayCoDon, I've been in contact with you before using the name embeddedthought. My role has been focused towards conducting analysis of Peercoin's underlying economic model and providing insight for long-term projections.
Sentinelrv:	I like to pass this meme around in regards to Peerbox.
Sentinelrv:	http://i.imgur.com/LSeqOaX.png_3 *(see image next page)*
peerchemist:	oh and I also package binaries for Ubuntu/ArchLinux and other distros. I could use some interest in that field (users)
hrobeers:	@JayCoDon, I guess it's close enough ;)

JayCoDon:	@saeveritt Ahh, you're the guy who kept reminding me that there were posts on my thread. Thanks, mate!
saeveritt:	@JayCoDon, Anytime ;)
Sentinelrv:	saeveritt is also creating Peercoin Wisdom here: ...
JayCoDon:	Very cool.
saeveritt:	Thanks Sentinelrv for grabbing the link.
Sentinelrv:	PeerAssets link is here ...
Sentinelrv:	And Peerbox: ...
JayCoDon:	Alright, so let's start from the top. From a mining perspective, after Bitcoin's halving, the hashrate spiked quite significantly, from ~500TH to over 3.5PH. That has since dropped back done. My understanding on the distribution of new peercoin is that it is based entirely on difficulty. 1. Am I right about that? 2. Can you (anyone) talk to how the hashrate fluctuates in comparison to what the difficulty is?
Sunny King:	yes it's based on proof-of-work difficulty

saeveritt:	To give you a visual representation of how BTC's halving affected PPC's coinbase reward I've prepared this graph:
JayCoDon:	But with bitcoin, the reward is constant. Is peercoin's dynamic?
Sunny King:	we talk about proof-of-work difficulty here as there is another proof-of-stake difficulty in peercoin
Sunny King:	the difficulty adjusts gradually every block, to make the average 10-minute block interval
JayCoDon:	The PoW doesn't actually do anything to secure the network, right? That's the PoS aspect?
peerchemist:	PoW is distributing coins
peerchemist:	proof of fiat burn
peerchemist:	PoS is for security
Sunny King:	in the case of the halving event of bitcoin, our difficulty adjusted upward, but slower than the spike of mining of course
JayCoDon:	I have heard complaints about PoS not being as secure of PoW. You've staked your currency's security on that. Why are the concerns about PoS being not secure unfounded?
peerchemist:	Peercoin has proven that PoS can secure the network, it is around for almost 4 years
Sunny King:	I think both systems have uncertainties, proof-of-stake is a more complex technology, we think it's competitive to PoW security wise
hrobeers:	If a fair distribution mechanism is used (PoW) the network is more decentralised. We don't have all our chain securing power localised in some regions with cheap electricity.
JayCoDon:	So by using a PoS mechanism, electricity isn't an issue, thus allowing for more decentralisation?
peerchemist:	exactly

saeveritt: To answer your question on the dynamic reward: Rather than waiting an arbitrary X amount of blocks for reward reduction, peercoin's coinbase reward is inversely related to difficulty. This lets the market decide when to reduce supply and it will naturally decouple Peercoin from other competition that is not as adaptable.

JayCoDon: To follow up on that saeveritt, there can be different amounts of coin created each day, but on the average spread out across days/weeks/months, it's about the same?

hrobeers: Don't forget that it is key to distribute the coins fairly, a large IPO where the developers hold a large portion of the Stake is a security risk.

JayCoDon: Oh, I completely agree with that @hrobeers

hrobeers: That's where we use PoW for, just like bitcoin.

hrobeers: The amount of coins created is largely dependent on the PoW difficulty

JayCoDon: As difficulty goes up, reward goes down; vice versa?

hrobeers: correct

JayCoDon: So pre-bitcoin halving, miners were earning more coins than post-halving?

Sunny King: that's right

saeveritt: JayCoDon, Yes there can be different amounts created each day. The spread out is about the same in terms of weeks but the average for a given period continually declines as time progresses due to increasing difficulty.

JayCoDon: So is there a pre-determined maximum?

hrobeers: I'll give sunny more chance to answer here, as it is his interview.

JayCoDon: You're all welcome to participate. I've got some good questions for Sunny later on ;)

Sunny King: yeah don't worry it's our interview :)

Sunny King: there is a preset maximum for the minimum difficulty of 1

JayCoDon:	And final question about mining before we move on: Is there a maximum number of Peercoin that will ever be released or, if mining gets to difficulty of 1, will it just be the 1% PoS reward?
JayCoDon:	So not true maximum, but a tightly controlled inflation rate that people can verify
hrobeers:	correct
hrobeers:	the transaction fees are burned
hrobeers:	so we can even get deflation
JayCoDon:	So 1% growth, but all fees are burned, which should counteract that 1% growth. That's interesting.
saeveritt:	Eventually the reward from PoW mining will converge towards 0. After this all that will be left is the ~1% annual inflation. There is a 0.01 ppc/kb fee for every transaction that is destroyed that helps counter the inflation
JayCoDon:	Very cool. Alright, I understand those mechanics now.
JayCoDon:	Next question: Why peercoin over another cryptocurrency, primarily bitcoin?
peerchemist:	but lets be fair and say that mining will probably never stp, diff will always be above 0
hrobeers:	so you pay per use of the network, but you don't pay the miner, you pay the network. (0.01ppc/kb)
hrobeers:	mining will never stop indeed
peerchemist:	Peercoin was my first crypto, as it seemed fair (unlike Bitcoin). Simple answer here.
JayCoDon:	What makes bitcoin unfair?
Sentinelrv:	NXT for example uses PoS, but their security model is determined by gaining fees. That becomes a problem when the majority of transactions are on exchanges where no transaction fees are paid. Peercoin has a more consistent security model in that it does not rely of fees. They are instead destroyed.

peerchemist: that is how it seemed to me back then in early 2014. It was just felt too centralised, as in big miners rule everything

peerchemist: now I know far more, but that was my inspiration on why to enter PPC instead of any other crypto

JayCoDon: What problem does peercoin solve that a different cryptocurrency couldn't?

peerchemist: decentralisation of the control over the network

saeveritt: JayCoDon, To add to Sentinelrv's comparison to the other widely known PoS, NXT. For PPC there remains consistent incentive to secure the network in terms of the ~1% minting reward. The NXT network relies on its fee structure as incentive. With NXT, almost all transactions are done off chain and on exchanges so incentive to secure the network is dependent on fee volume. It's not reliable and that's why they need Ardor.

Sunny King: Actually peercoin solves several big problems

peerchemist: please continue Sunny

hrobeers: My reason for peercoin is that there isn't a large outflux of money due to mining. The mining cost is covered by the entire network after all.

hrobeers: yeah continue

Sunny King: One is that energy is not required to achieve decentralisation

Sunny King: Other is that it opens up the whole blockchain ecosystem, in that now ppl don't need mining power to jump start new blockchains

Sunny King: so in my opinion PoS is a huge step forward for blockchain tech

JayCoDon: From a participation perspective, what does the average person who may not even care about mining gain? What problems are solved from that perspective?

hrobeers: Let's say we want to use the network to distribute computing power. PoW would compete with the useful work for resources, which pumps up the price of the useful work.

hrobeers:	a bit like how biofuel competes with food production.
Sunny King:	It enables new applications to use its own blockchain much more cost effectively. For example, there is a peershare project in our community that enables any DAO to run it's own blockchain
Sentinelrv:	Yes Sunny, energy is used to distribute new currency fairly, however it is not required in order to secure the network, since PoS takes care of that by itself.
JayCoDon:	Is peercoin's single most important feature its PoS mechanism?
hrobeers:	it's economics are as important
JayCoDon:	Please elaborate.
peerchemist:	more important than PoS
peerchemist:	Peercoin innovated far more about "mining" actually
peerchemist:	Sunny please elaborate on how was mining reward algorithm was chosen. Moore's Law and all.
Sunny King:	Yeah the mining rate and curve is designed more naturally than bitcoin's, but I would agree that proof-of-stake is the single most important contribution to blockchain technology in general
hrobeers:	can you explain the parallel with Moore's Law?
Sunny King:	basically like saeveritt said earlier, mining rate is inversely related to difficulty. So if assuming Moore's Law, then the mining rate would continue to drop geometrically.
Sunny King:	In short, Moore's Law would ensure the PoW inflation to be similar to bitcoin's
JayCoDon:	As reward drops, PoW drops as well?
Sunny King:	No it's inversely related, difficulty goes up, reward drops
hrobeers:	but the same hashrate get's cheaper over time
JayCoDon:	I meant for bitcoin's
peerchemist:	what hrobeers said + due to Moore's Law
JayCoDon:	Ahh, okay.

saeveritt:	If we focus on what a store of value represents we must think long term about how different economic models will compete with one another. When a cryptocurrency that has a responsive economic model is in direct competition with one that is more rigid and pre-defined, the market will discover use case. We are just now seeing that PPC's current inflation rate is already lower than btc's. ltc's and nmc's will be by 2020. Dyna
Sunny King:	for bitcoin it's a different matter though, that's due to a lot of miners becoming unprofitable
JayCoDon:	Hence why they moved over to peercoin to begin with
hrobeers:	correct
peerchemist:	and PPC will allow them to be profitable for some more time, unlike BTC which sharply discards thm
hrobeers:	so coinbase reward drop, will lower the outflux of money for mining, unless if the price goes up accordingly.
JayCoDon:	I've heard miners talk about the shock of going from 25 to 12.5. Peercoin's more dynamic drop in reward as difficulty goes up is less shocking. Alright, I understand that.
JayCoDon:	Alright, changing topics 180 degress. What is Peercoin's approach to hard forks? As we've seen with Bitcoin/Ethereum, they have taken two very different approaches with the former being ardently against while the latter has forked because of a hack.
peerchemist:	we were just discussing that while waiting for you. Due to PoS, our chain does wherever big holders (big stakers) want it to go
Sunny King:	I think we are more flexible than bitcoin in this respect
Sunny King:	we typically run an upgrade window less than 3 months
JayCoDon:	Interesting. @peerchemist … Isn't the big holders controlling the destiny a risk of PoS?
Sunny King:	so for incompatible upgrade, users have a couple months before they are on a unsupported fork
JayCoDon:	@sunnyking Do you not allow for soft forks at all?

hrobeers:	big holders have interest in well being of chain, unlike the big miners
peerchemist:	it is fundamental tradeoff. With PoW you outsource the security and flexibility to third parties to prevent big holders from "taking control" and with PoS you keep the security within the system and rely on economic sanity of "big holders"
saeveritt:	Much less of a risk than what a conglomeration of centralised miners pose due to the holders having stake in the network.
JayCoDon:	But in the instance where a DAO like hack occurred, the big holders could ruin Peercoin's immutable nature by forking because they were likely impacted the most, no?
peerchemist:	in the case of ETH/DAO I guess our stakers would react the same, yes
JayCoDon:	I'm asking because we see that with Ethereum 2/3rd of the ETH in the DAO were early mined Ether, so they were obviously incentivised to hard fork to get their money back
peerchemist:	* same as ETH miners
Sunny King:	There might be such possibility, that big holder want to participate in the decision making of upgrades. So far we haven't encountered such a problem
saeveritt:	It's a question of whether the majority of stakers share the same incentive to bailout a DAO type organisation.
JayCoDon:	Wouldn't they because they likely are in that DAO?
JayCoDon:	2/3rd of ETH in DAO were majority stakers.
peerchemist:	interesting JayCoDon, than in that case it could get interesting if so many "old coins" are stolen as then the smaller fish would dominate the staking for a while and could fork the chain. Due to the destruction of so many coin days
JayCoDon:	Hmm … Interesting.
hrobeers:	:)
JayCoDon:	Alright, here's my "tough" question for Sunny
peerchemist:	omg :O

saeveritt:	:)
hrobeers:	losing your coins, results in losing your power
saeveritt:	and soul
peerchemist:	coin days are just as important
saeveritt:	most definitely
hrobeers:	correct
JayCoDon:	Sunny, you're the Satoshi or Vitalik of Peercoin. You're the "benevolent" dictator of it. People follow you. I am of the opinion that the reason Bitcoin has been so successful is because Satoshi went away; because that founder went away, so he couldn't influence decisions. You likely are a big stake holder and undo political pressure could force you to do things that are not in the best interest of Peercoin.
JayCoDon:	even though the fork was probably not the right thing to do. Do you believe that make you a potential security risk?
Sunny King:	Satoshi is surprising, I actually don't mind giving more and more power away to other capable community members, I think that's also healthy to the development of the project
Sunny King:	though I don't plan to disappear suddenly like Satoshi did
Sunny King:	It's a bit strange that you abandon such a brilliant invention so completely?
peerchemist:	yeah, you will just slowly fade to 0
Sunny King:	at least I have a bit trouble understanding
peerchemist:	unlike satoshi, who went from 1 to 0 in a single block
hrobeers:	The community is also innovating outside the core protocol and Sunny is doing a great job, so there is no reason to overthrow him.
JayCoDon:	Are there safeguards in place in the event that Sunny King does disappear?
JayCoDon:	A sort o "passing the torch" akin to Satoshi and Gavin?
hrobeers:	Some developers have knowledge of the PoS workings and are able to sustain development

hrobeers:	but the code is very close to the bitcoin code.
peerchemist:	why did no one understand my joke about Sunny not leaving at once but slowly fading to 0? :(
JayCoDon:	Peerchemist, I have it noted to try to fit that into my piece ;)
Sentinelrv:	Like Sigmike, who is also a core developer
Sunny King:	The main issue is competent leaders that can take over in such case
peerchemist:	yeah, Peercoin is "cheap" to maintain
hrobeers:	:) parallel to PoW :p
peerchemist:	yep!
hrobeers:	we have a handful of developers that contributed to the code and are capable to continue the work.
saeveritt:	peerchemist, I did :) Thought it was funny because bitcoins reward drops abruptly like Satoshi and peercoins declines slowly over time ;)
peerchemist:	oh sorry I thought you've missed it out
peerchemist:	but I would like to note that we lack devs
hrobeers:	I for example run a modified ppc client on my peerbox.
peerchemist:	devs who could handle bigger projects
peerchemist:	we have just enough devs to keep the lights on, not to evolve into something bigger
Sentinelrv:	This question can also be related to synchronised checkpoints, which critics of proof-of-stake say is used to keep Peercoin network running correctly. Sunny controls the keys to checkpoints, so the network is dependent on him at the moment I feel.
Sentinelrv:	I think we should talk about that, as checkpoints will soon become optional with v0.6.
hrobeers:	it isn't, the community can already ditch checkpoints today at any time. It will just become more simple
Sentinelrv:	Also, one of our Peershares networks Nu has run without checkpoints since September 2014 with no trouble.

JayCoDon:	Can you quickly explain what these checkpoints are?
peerchemist:	Sunny, pls
Sunny King:	yeah there isn't anything that I control that cannot be overridden via an upgrade
hrobeers:	it's a common misconception. Sunny you explain checkpoints?
Sentinelrv:	It is one of the main criticisms of PoS, so I felt it should be addressed.
Sunny King:	the checkpoint system is an additional temporary safeguard
saeveritt:	As I understand it, checkpoints were only needed for ensuring network security during the first couple months where security was PoW dependent during the initial distribution before PoS security took over
Sunny King:	it definitely needs it as it's too easy to attack PoW new blockchain
JayCoDon:	And what were the checkpoints specifically?
Sunny King:	peercoin's PoS only turns on after one month
hrobeers:	checkpoints are a way for Sunny to broadcast attacks on the chain
peerchemist:	checkpoints are pointers to "correct" version of the chain and can be used to reconfigure a network in case of major problem
Sunny King:	it synchronise the network, basically "freeze" the blockchain so it cannot reorg beyond it
hrobeers:	so that clients can follow Sunny's advice not to follow the incorrect chain
Sunny King:	just like the hard checkpoint in bitcoin, but it's not coded into the source but broadcasted from a privileged node
hrobeers:	but a client implementation can easily ignore the checkpoints from the point they get abused
JayCoDon:	So if Sunny King abuses those checkpoints, the client implementation can just ignore.
hrobeers:	clients should actively chose to ignore them

peerchemist:	yes, just then someone who is not the sunny must build the binaries and help to deploy them. For example I could switch over all Peerbox nodes in about 15 min to version who ignores sunny and his checkpoints
JayCoDon:	Very interesting.
hrobeers:	same would be true for peerkeeper backend (once in browser minting is implemented)
Sunny King:	It was kept for a while as we also want the coins to distribute more evently, avoid possibility of 51% attack, also other vulnerabilities
saeveritt:	yes network security has definitely hardened thanks to continual distribution
Sunny King:	but in any case it was never an essential part of the design so it can be disabled freely
JayCoDon:	Final question. The market cap has stayed relatively constant over the past few months at ~8-10 million marketcap. What does peercoin need for it to start increasing in valuation again?
hrobeers:	that's a common misconception on the internet, that checkpoints centralise the network. But the DAO hard fork has shown that abuse is just as easy without checkpoints.
peerchemist:	Peercoin needs fresh blood, more developers, more ideas
Sunny King:	I think the community is doing great projects, that's the most important aspects. We grow the ecosystem, make it more useful for all kinds of purposes
peerchemist:	but if we can sustain 10M cap, then let is be. I choose that over bloated 150M cap which just awaits to burst
Sunny King:	then the market would reflect
hrobeers:	there are hug bubbles going on, we prefer to build a sustainable chain

Sentinelrv: I believe we need more project development around Peercoin like PeerAssets. Peerchemist, if you'd like, cold you explain you project and why you believe it will bring more value to Peercoin, including the fact that it will help with deflation of the supply.

hrobeers: it is capable of surviving a second internet bubble

peerchemist: I can explain, but I guess that is best to be left for some other time

saeveritt: I believe all that it needs is time. If you reference the graph I linked to earlier there is a significant drop in block reward from May 2015 to the end of July 2015. If you look at the subsequent price response the cycle becomes apparent. During this time Peercoin went from $0.21 to a high of $0.75. The market determined that with the new reduction in supply, the price would average around $0.40 and has maintained that for since PPC has reached a stage of maturity (thank you btc halving) to where it's block reward has encountered another significant drop that mirrors the may 2015 fall, I believe we will find a new price floor very soon and it will correlate with the percentage change in reward

hrobeers: The point is that many coins are killed these days by investors and big money

peerchemist: ie, thanks to our economic model we do not have to run to get new fancy features and keep the speculation bubble going. We are running a marathon, and we are always close to the top even in this early days

hrobeers: Ethereum being the perfect example

saeveritt: Yes, economic models designed to endure bubbles and adapt to fluctuating market pressures will show longevity

JayCoDon: Very good. This should be good enough for now; this was really enlightening. If I have further questions, I'll send them to Sentinelrv to get them answered.

peerchemist:	also sanity of Peercoin is attracting the right minds, at least it seems so to me
hrobeers:	I have one thing I'd like to add as developer
JayCoDon:	Sure, go ahead
hrobeers:	This is key for me: The decentralization makes it possible for everyone to mint a block from time to time. This simplifies experimentation with non-standard txns on the network. This helps innovation.
saeveritt:	Enjoyed the questions, Jacob. Thank you.
hrobeers:	I'm impressed by the questions, they were very good indeed.
peerchemist:	I am glad I have participated, cu around Jacob
Sunny King:	Thanks Jacob for a great conversation
Sentinelrv:	"The right minds" Yes, I always feel as if peercoin always attracts the most level headed and logical people compared to most other crypto communities.
JayCoDon:	And just to make one point: I know everyone is excited about CoinDesk writing about this, but I make no promises. I have a tentative yes from my editor, but until he sees the piece, nothing is for sure. But I'll do my best. :)
hrobeers:	:)
saeveritt:	:)
Sunny King:	appreciate it :)
JayCoDon:	Talk soon, guys.
hrobeers:	Thank Jacob, I think I have to take a subscription to your articles.
Sentinelrv:	Thanks!
Sunny King:	Thanks everyone :)
Sentinelrv:	So how did it go you think?
peerchemist:	that went well
peerchemist:	I think we have suceeded in what I have wanted to do
peerchemist:	to give out a fresh image of Peercoin, a community of smart and passionate people
hrobeers:	I'm happy :)
hrobeers:	we gave it our best shot.
peerchemist:	yeah I think we gave him enough to write a damn good story
Sunny King:	I think it's probably one of the best participated meetings we have ever did

hrobeers: I can't imagine how we could have done better

Sunny King: everyone is well heard :)

Sentinelrv: And we should do more I think.
saeveritt: I enjoyed reading all of your responses and answering as well:)

hrobeers: we also sounded like a team

Sentinelrv: I will ask Jacob if we could possibly post the chat publicly if/ after his article is released.

hrobeers: I'm off

hrobeers: cu guys

Sunny King: bye hrobeers

Sunny King: I need to go too, peerchemist I will drop you email later

Sentinelrv: See you Sunny.

saeveritt: Bye Sunny. Enjoyed the chat. :)

Sunny King: thanks guys enjoyed the meeting very much :)

Sunny King: talk to you soon

peerchemist: cu sunny